More Teacher Gifts

COMPILED BY Barbara Delaney

interweave.com

Interweave grants permission to photocopy the templates in this publication for personal use.

The projects in this collection were originally published in other Interweave publications, including 101 Patchwork, Modern Patchwork, Quilt Scene, Quilting Arts, *and* Stitch *magazines. Some have been altered to update information and/or conform to space limitations.*

Interweave
A division of F+W Media, Inc.
201 East Fourth Street
Loveland, CO 80537
interweave.com

Manufactured in the United States by Versa Press

ISBN 978-1-62033-560-4 (pbk.)

Contents

Artsy Apron

BY JEANNIE PALMER MOORE

Why not customize an apron for everyone on your list? It's a nostalgic gift that brings to mind such good memories of baking in the kitchen. The vision of my Grandma Alice in her apron is so vivid that it always makes me smile. You can recycle old denim, layer screen-printed paint on fabric, or use any surface design techniques that you like to create the fabric for your apron. I've designed two different aprons that can be modified with ruffles, trim, embellishments, and pockets. The directions and patterns differ for the skirt fronts, but the waistbands and ties are the same for both aprons.

Materials

For both aprons

☐ Photocopy machine and paper

☐ Fabric paints, silk-screen printing materials, Thermofax screens, Procion MX dyes, or any other surface design materials you like

☐ Sewing machine with free-motion stitching capabilities

☐ Sewing-machine thread in a coordinating color

☐ Handsewing needle and thread

☐ Rotary cutter, mat, and acrylic ruler

☐ Fabric scissors

☐ Pins

☐ Iron and ironing board

For the red painted apron

☐ Fabric for the apron front, 36" × 24" (91.5 × 61 cm)

☐ Backing fabric, 22" × 33" (56 × 84 cm)

☐ Batting, 22" × 33" (56 × 84 cm)

☐ Waistband fabric, 5" × 20" (12.5 × 51 cm)

☐ Fabric for the ties, two 4" × 32" (10 × 81.5 cm) strips

☐ Fabric for a pocket

☐ Template on page 7

For the indigo apron

☐ Fabric(s) for the apron front, 21" × 16" (53.5 × 40.5 cm) (see Steps 9 and 10 in the "Indigo Apron" instructions)

☐ Backing fabric, 21" × 16" (53.5 × 40.5 cm)

☐ Waistband fabric, 5" × 20" (12.5 × 51 cm)

☐ Fabric for the ties, two 4" × 32" (10 × 81.5 cm) strips

☐ Fabric for the ruffle, 4" × 67" (10 × 170 cm)

☐ Template on page 7

Optional (for the indigo apron)

☐ Batting, 21" × 16" (53.5 × 40.5 cm)

☐ Scraps of cheesecloth and fibers

☐ Needle-felting machine

☐ Fabric for a pocket

Red Painted Apron

1 Photocopy the pattern piece provided on page 7, enlarging it by 290%.

2 Use a silk screen or fabric paints to create the fabric for the apron front, waistband, pocket, and ties. For my apron, I painted a wholecloth piece with 5 layers in the following sequence:

— 1st layer: Silk-screen circle print with silver paint

— 2nd layer: Thermofax flower print with red and pink paint

— 3rd layer: Thermofax dot print with yellow paint

— 4th layer: Thermofax script print with gray paint

— 5th layer: Silk-screen brush print with beige paint

3 Thoroughly dry all of the painted layers and iron and/or wash the fabric to soften it.

4 Use the pattern pieces to cut 10 strips of fabric. Rearrange the strips and sew them together along their long edges to form the apron front.

5 Trim the backing piece and batting to match the top piece. Lay the backing piece and the finished top piece with their right sides together. Lay the batting on either wrong side of the fabric sandwich. Pin all three layers together and stitch around the perimeter, leaving the top band open for turning.

6 Cut the points, turn the apron right-side out, and press. Free-motion stitch all three layers.

7 See directions for "Finishing Both Aprons."

Indigo Apron

8 Photocopy the pattern provided on page 7, enlarging it by 220%.

9 Use whatever surface design techniques you like to decorate fabrics for the apron front and waistband. You can even paint a pocket from an old pair of jeans to use as the pocket on your apron.

Note: To create my apron, I used strips of shibori-dyed fabrics, old denim that I screen printed with white and silver paint, and organza newsprint fabric.

10 Assemble your fabrics to create a wholecloth piece that measures approximately 21" × 16" (53.5 × 40.5 cm). After piecing fabrics together to create my base, I used a needle-felting machine to embellish the surface with organza newsprint fabric, cheescloth, and fibers. You could also use a sewing machine to add additional fabrics and fibers to the surface of your base fabric.

11 Fold your wholecloth piece in half along the long edge, right sides facing. Line up the long straight edge of the pattern piece with the folded edge of the fabric, trace the pattern piece, and cut it out with the fabric still folded so you have a symmetrical apron front. Cut a piece of backing fabric (and batting, if desired) in the same way.

12 For the ruffle, cut a strip of fabric 1½ times the length of the apron perimeter (minus the top edge) by 4" (10 cm) wide. It will be approximately 4" × 67" (10 × 170 cm). Fold the strip in half lengthwise with the wrong sides together, and sew a running stitch. Gather the fabric to create a ruffle the length of the perimeter. Pin the raw edge of the ruffle to the front of the apron, right sides facing, so that the folded edge of the ruffle is lying on the apron front. Stitch the ruffle to the apron using a scant ¼" (6 mm) seam allowance.

13 With the ruffle still lying against the top piece, lay the backing piece onto the top piece, right sides together. Pin and stitch the top and back piece together along the curved edge, leaving the top band open for turning.

Note: I did not include a layer of batting in my denim skirt, but if you choose to do so, pin it to either wrong side of the sandwich before sewing.

14 Turn the apron right-side out, press, and free-motion stitch the layers.

15 See directions for "Finishing Both Aprons."

Finishing Both Aprons

16 Measure the top band of your apron. Cut a piece of waistband fabric 1" (2.5 cm) longer than this length by 5" (12.5 cm) wide, approximately 5" × 20" (12.5 × 51 cm).

17 Turn under the short raw edges of the waistband ½" (1.3 cm) on each end so the waistband lines up with the skirt top. Turn under the bottom long edge of the waistband ½" (1.3 cm) and press. Note that the top edge remains raw.

18 Align the top long edge of the waistband with the top edge of the apron front, right sides facing, and stitch the two pieces together.

19 Fold the waistband over to the back side of the apron. Pin and baste stitch the waistband to the back side of the apron, leaving the short ends open.

20 Fold each of the 4" × 32" (10 × 81.5 cm) strips with right sides together. If you like, you can trim one of the short ends of each strip at an angle to form the end of the apron tie.

21 Stitch each folded strip along its long side and one short end, leaving the other end open. Turn the ties right-side out and press.

22 Place the open ends of the ties into the waistband openings at each end and stitch them in place.

23 Sew on the pocket of your choice. For the red painted apron, I cut out two 6" (15 cm) squares, and stitched them together with right sides facing, using a ¼" (6 mm) seam allowance. I turned the square right-side out, folded down one of the corners, and attached the square to the apron front with a zigzag stitch, leaving the folded corner unstitched at the top for the pocket opening. ✎

- -

JEANNIE PALMER MOORE continues to explore the processes of dyeing, printing, and painting in order to create her art quilts. She resides in the San Diego area where she often demonstrates her techniques. See more of her work at jpmartist.com.

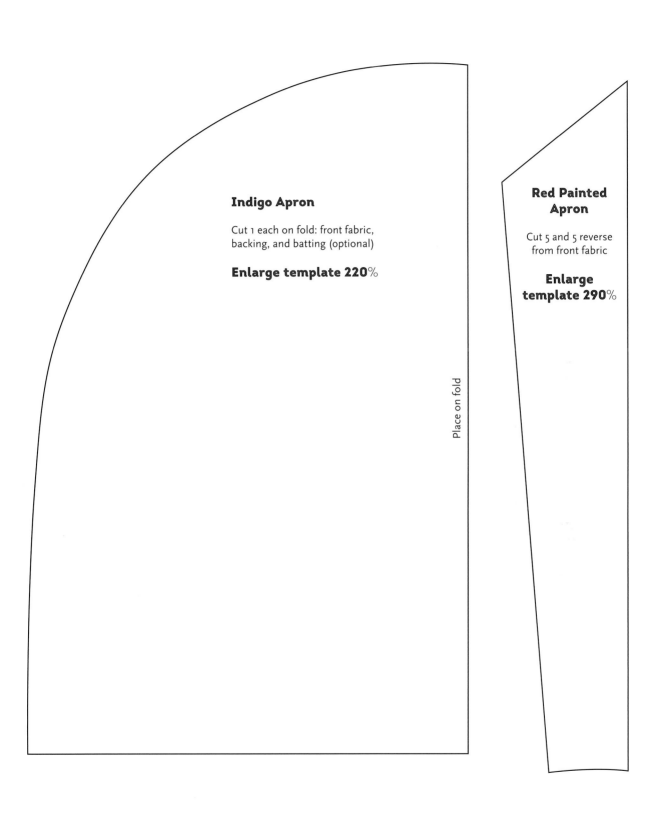

Indigo Apron

Cut 1 each on fold: front fabric, backing, and batting (optional)

Enlarge template 220%

Place on fold

Red Painted Apron

Cut 5 and 5 reverse from front fabric

Enlarge template 290%

Materials

- ¼ yd (23 cm) of 36" (91 cm) wide or wider wool felt (Main; shown: muted maroon)

- Scraps of wool felt in 4 different colors (assign each color a number, 1–4; shown: pink [#1], muted yellow [#2], dark sage green [#3], and light sage green [#4])

- ¼ yd (23 cm) insulated batting (such as Insul-Bright from The Warm Company)

- ⅛ yd (11.5 cm) fusible web

- Brown embroidery floss

- Press cloth

- Hand-embroidery needle

- Stepping-Stones Pot Holder templates on page 10

Finished Size

7¼" (18.5 cm) diameter

Notes

* Follow the manufacturer's instructions when using the fusible web. However, you may want to use steam to help the heat penetrate through the thick felt, even if the manufacturer recommends a dry iron.

* Feel free to mix felted wool of different textures, including wool recycled from felted clothing. Just be sure not to use acrylic felt if you want a functional pot holder, because the heat from a dish could melt it.

Stepping-Stones Pot Holder

BY KEVIN KOSBAB

The wool "stones" on this felt pot holder aren't just for show—they add an extra layer to protect your table from heat. The appliqué circles are attached with fusible web and finished by hand with a simple blanket stitch.

Cut Fabric

1 Trace and cut 2 of template A from the Main felt. Cut a 5" × ½" (12.5 × 1.3 cm) strip from the Main felt. Cut 1 of template F from the insulated batting.

2 Trace the remaining templates onto the paper side of fusible web, tracing the number indicated below. Be sure to leave at least ½" (1.3 cm) between circles.

— 3 of template B

— 5 of template C

— 5 of template D

— 2 of template E

3 Cut out the fusible web circles roughly ¼" (6 mm) outside the lines. Following the manufacturer's instructions, press the web to the wrong side of the felt scraps as indicated (or as desired).

— From felt #1: 1 each of B, C, D, and E

— From felt #2: 1 of B, 2 of D

— From felt #3: 3 of C, 1 of D

— From felt #4: 1 each of B, C, D, and E

4 Cut the fused felt circles along the lines.

Attach Circle Appliqués

5 Peel the paper backings from the fused felt circles. Arrange the circles, fusible-side down, on one of the Main A pieces, referring to the diagram opposite for guidance on placement. Press with a steam iron to adhere the circle appliqués to the Main piece. *Note: Cover the felt with a press cloth to help avoid a shiny appearance from the heat of fusing.*

6 Using 2 strands of embroidery floss and the hand-embroidery needle, blanket-stitch around each of the circle appliqués.

Assemble Pot Holder

7 Center the batting circle on the wrong side of the remaining Main circle, then place the appliquéd Main circle on top right-side up, so the batting is sandwiched between the circles. Pin around the perimeter. To make a hanging loop,

fold the 5" × ½" (12.5 × 1.3 cm) Main felt strip in half and insert both ends between the layers of felt, overlapping the ends and inserting about ½" (1.3 cm) between the layers. Pin the strip in place.

8 Again using 2 strands of embroidery floss, blanket-stitch securely around the Main pieces to attach them to each other, enclosing the batting and catching the hanging loop in the stitches. ✏

- -

KEVIN KOSBAB is a writer, an editor, and a pattern designer. His modern quilts and sewing projects have appeared in *Stitch*, and his Feed Dog Designs patterns are available on the Web at feeddog.net.

Pot Holder Color Key

- #1 (pink)
- #2 (muted yellow)
- #3 (dark sage green)
- #4 (light sage green)

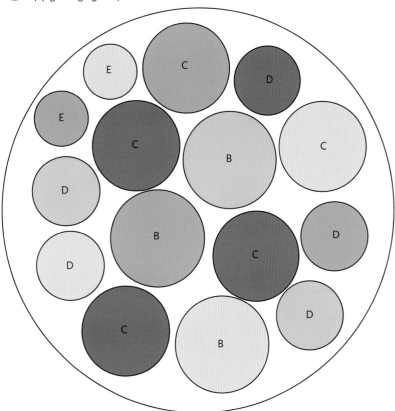

Templates are actual size

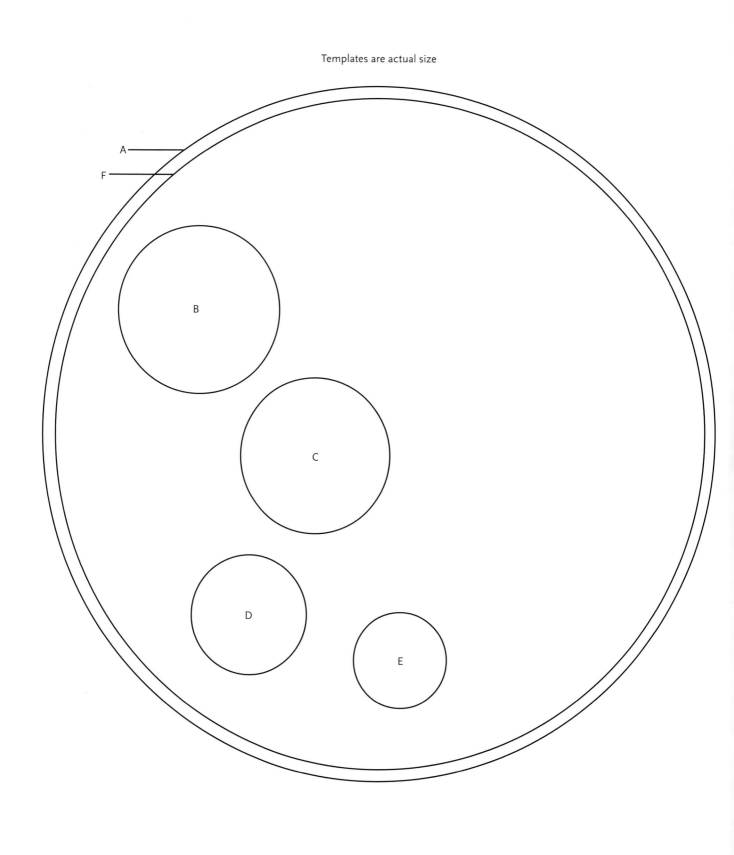

Retro Kitchen Set

BY JENNIFER REYNOLDS

There is an old saying that red and green should never be seen together, but this lime-green and red fruit-embellished tea towel and apron set is sure to make you want to combine them. Using store-bought tea towels as the base fabric simplifies the project, and the vivid appliqué details and handstitching will brighten any kitchen.

Materials

See Notes for more fabric information.

☐ Three 19¼" × 27½" (49 × 70 cm) tea towels (Main; shown: white waffle weave) or 1⅔ yd (1.2 m) of 45" (114.5 cm) wide cotton toweling fabric

☐ 1 fat eighth each of 2 different colors of tonal or solid fabric (A and B; shown: deep orange and red)

☐ 1 fat eighth of print fabric (C; shown: green and white)

☐ 1 fat quarter plus an 8" (20.5 cm) square or ¾ yd (69 cm) of print fabric (D; shown: green and yellow)

☐ 8" (20.5 cm) square of tonal or solid fabric (E; shown: green)

☐ 5" (12.5 cm) square of print fabric (F; shown: red and white)

☐ 2" (5 cm) square of a different print fabric in same or similar color as previous listing (G; shown: red-on-red print)

☐ 12" (30.5 cm) square of double-sided fusible web (such as Steam-A-Seam)

☐ 1 skein each of 2 different colors of embroidery floss (shown: DMC 6-strand embroidery floss, 666 [red] and 907 [lime])

☐ Sewing thread in colors to match the Main and contrast fabrics (shown: white, red, and lime green)

☐ Embroidery needle

☐ 3 yd (2.7 m) of ½" (1.3 cm) wide cotton twill tape

☐ Rotary cutter, rigid acrylic ruler, and self-healing mat

☐ Pencil or water-soluble fabric marker

☐ Point turner or chopstick

☐ Retro Kitchen Set templates on page 15

Finished Size

Apron is 19¼" at widest point × 27½" long (49 × 70 cm) and is adjustable with tie. Towels are 19¼" wide × 26¾" long (49 × 68 cm).

Notes

✳ All seam allowances are ¼" (6 mm) unless otherwise noted.

✳ Here is the fabric breakdown as shown in the sample:
A: orange tonal fabric for the pear tea towel appliqué background panel
B: red tonal fabric for the apron pocket and apple appliqués
C: bright green and white floral print for the pear appliqués and apron pocket lining
D: pale lime green and yellow floral print for the apple tea towel appliqué background panel, pear appliqués, 5 pear appliqué leaves, apron pocket trim, bottom band of the apron, and pocket lining
E: lime green tonal fabric for pear appliqués and 1 pear leaf appliqué
F: red and white multisize polka-dot print for apple appliqués
G: red-on-red floral print fabric for 2 apple appliqué leaves

✳ Fat quarters and fat eighths are fabric cuts often sold (alone or in color-coordinated sets) at fabric and quilt stores. Fat quarters are generally 18" × 22" (45.5 × 56 cm); fat eighths are generally 9" × 22" (21 × 56 cm).

✳ If you find towels that you like and they are not the exact size as those listed here, simply measure the width of your towels after you have prewashed them to allow for shrinkage. Add 1" (2.5 cm) to the width measurement to allow for hemming the sides of the appliqué background panel and the accent border at the bottom of the apron.

✳ If you purchase cotton toweling instead of finished cotton towels, the yardage listed allows for 10 to 12 percent shrinkage and for hemming raw edges.

✳ Prewash and press the towels and fabrics.

✳ The appliqué template pieces are already reversed for use with the fusible web.

Cut the Fabric

1 Cut the following pieces as directed.

From fabric A:

— 5¾" × 21" (14.5 × 53.5 cm) strip for the Pear Tea Towel Appliqué Background Panel

From fabric B:

— 7¾" × 9" (19.5 × 23 cm) rectangle for the Apron Pocket

From fabric C:

— 8½" × 9" (21.5 × 23 cm) rectangle for the Apron Pocket Lining

From fabric D:

— 5¾" × 21" (14.5 × 53.5 cm) strip for the Apple Tea Towel Appliqué Background Panel

— 2" × 21" (5 × 53.5 cm) strip for the Accent Border at the bottom of the Apron

— 1¼" × 9" (3.2 × 23 cm) strip for the Accent Strip at the top of the Apron Pocket

The remaining fabric will be used for the appliqués.

2 Cut the cotton twill tape into the following lengths:

— Two 26" (66 cm) lengths

— Two 25" (63.5 cm) lengths

Set aside all the cut pieces.

Prepare the Appliqués

3 Use a pencil to trace the following onto the paper side of the fusible web, leaving at least ½" (1.3 cm) between each shape:

— 1 Large Apple and 1 Large Apple Center

— 1 Small Apple and 1 Small Apple Center

— 2 Large Pears and 2 Large Pear Centers

— 2 Small Pears and 2 Small Pear Centers

— 2 Large and 2 Small Apple Leaves

— 3 Large and 3 Small Pear Leaves

4 Cut out each shape, leaving a ¼" (6 mm) margin around each shape.

5 Following the manufacturer's instructions, fuse the 2 Large Pears and the 2 Small Pear Centers onto the wrong side of fabric C.

6 Fuse all 6 Pear Leaves (3 Large and 3 Small) onto the wrong side of fabric D.

7 Fuse the Small Pears and the Large Pear Centers onto the wrong side of fabric E.

8 Fuse the Large Apple and the Small Apple Center onto the wrong side of fabric F.

9 Fuse the Large Apple Center and the Small Apple onto the wrong side of fabric B.

10 Fuse the 2 Apple Leaves onto the wrong side of fabric G.

11 Cut out each shape on the drawn lines.

Make the Apple Tea Towel

12 Place the 5¾" × 21" (14.5 × 53.5 cm) fabric D Background Panel right-side up on your work surface. Referring to the photo above, position the Large and Small Apples, Apple Centers, and the four Apple Leaves slightly to left of center (across the width) of the Panel. Leave 1" (2.5 cm) of empty space above the top of the Apple Leaves, to allow for hemming the top edge of the Panel. When you are pleased with your arrangement, remove the paper backing from the Large Apple and Small Apple and fuse the pieces in place. Let the pieces cool. Next, remove the paper backing and fuse the corresponding Apple Centers in place, then the Leaves.

13 Freehand draw the apple stems onto the Background Panel and on the outside of the Apple Centers with light pencil lines.

14 Hand embroider around the perimeter of the Apple Centers with two strands of contrasting embroidery thread (shown: lime green) with blanket stitches. Blanket-stitch around the Apples and the Leaves with two strands of matching embroidery thread (shown: green).

15 Using two strands of matching embroidery thread (shown: red), chain-stitch the part of the stem that sits on top of the Apples (and between each Apple's Leaves). Chain-stitch the stem that lies outside the Apple Centers with two strands of a contrasting embroidery thread (shown: red).

16 Cut the hem off one end of a tea towel with a rotary cutter. If you are working with waffle-weave towels, make sure you keep the lines of the waffle weave straight as you cut.

17 Lay the right side of the appliquéd panel down onto the wrong side of the tea towel, aligning the raw edge of the bottom of the towel with the raw edge at the bottom of the appliquéd panel. Check to make sure that the stems of the apple appliqués point toward the top of the towel. The two short sides of the appliqué panel will extend beyond the width of the towel.

18 With thread to match the towel, machine stitch the pieces together along the bottom edge. Press the seam allowances toward the appliquéd panel.

19 To create the side hems on both side edges of the appliquéd panel, press ½" (1.3 cm) toward the wrong side of the panel. Make sure the folded edges align with the side edges of the towel. If not, adjust the fold to match, then press again.

20 Press a hem into the edge at the top of the appliquéd panel, by folding ½" (1.3 cm) toward the wrong side of the panel.

21 Fold the appliquéd panel over so that the wrong side of the appliquéd panel faces the right side of the tea towel, aligning the folded and pressed side hems with the side edges of the towel. Smooth the pieces together so that both layers lie flat. Pin the side edges and top hemmed edge in place.

22 Thread your machine with thread to match the appliquéd panel. The bobbin should contain thread to match the towel (shown: white). Beginning at the bottom edge of the left-hand side, edgestitch the panel to the towel, a scant ⅛" (3 mm) from the panel's folded edges.

Make the Pear Tea Towel

23 Place the 5¾" × 21" (14.5 × 53.5 cm) fabric A Background Panel right-side up on your work surface. Referring to the photograph at left, position 1 Large Pear, 1 Small Pear, their corresponding Pear Centers, and 1 Large Pear Leaf and 1 Small Pear Leaf in the center (across the width) of the Panel. Leave ¾" (2 cm) of empty space above the top of the Pear Leaves, to allow for hemming the top edge of the Panel. When you are pleased with your arrangement, remove the paper backing from the Large and Small Pears and fuse them in place, as you did in Step 11. Next remove the paper backing and fuse the corresponding Pear Centers in place, then the Leaves.

24 Freehand draw the stems onto the Background Panel and on the outside of the Pear Centers with light pencil lines.

25 Hand embroider around the perimeter of the Pear Centers with two strands of contrasting embroidery thread (shown: red) with blanket stitches. Blanket-stitch around the perimeter of the Pears and Leaves with two strands of matching embroidery thread (shown: lime green) and blanket-stitch around the Pear Centers.

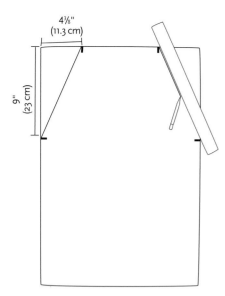

4⅜" (11.3 cm)

9" (23 cm)

diagram

26 Using two strands of matching embroidery thread (shown: lime green) chain-stitch the part of the stem that sits on top of the Pears (and between each Pear's Leaves). Chain-stitch the stem that lies outside the Pear Centers with two strands of a contrasting embroidery thread (shown: red).

27 Repeat Steps 15–21 to finish the tea towel.

Make the Apron

Refer to the diagram above for assistance with the following steps.

28 Lay the remaining tea towel on your work surface. On the top edge of the tea towel, measure 4⅜" (11.3 cm) from each side toward the center and make a light pencil mark.

29 Measure 9" (23 cm) down each side from the top edge and mark as before.

30 On the left-hand side of the towel, draw a line connecting the mark at the top edge of the tea towel to the mark on the side edge of the towel. Do the same on the right-hand side of the towel.

31 Using a rotary cutter and straight-edge, cut off the corners along the drawn lines.

32 Cut the hem off the bottom end of the towel with a rotary cutter. If you are working with waffle-weave towels, make sure you keep the lines of the

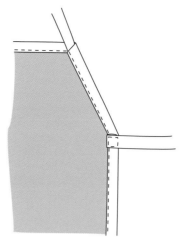

figure 1

waffle weave straight as you cut. You have created the apron front and now you are ready to embellish it with a pocket, accent bottom border, and, of course, the ties.

33 To hem the top edge of the apron's "bib," fold ¼" (6 mm) to the wrong side of the apron and press. Fold over the hem again ½" (1.3 cm) and press. Topstitch the hem in place, ⅜" (1 cm) from the outside edge, using matching thread (shown: white).

34 Prepare the hems for the two angled sides of the bib in the same manner used in Step 30. However, before you pin and sew them in place, with the apron facing wrong-side up, unfold the hems at the top corners of each angled side and place one end of each of the 25" (63.5 cm) lengths of twill tape at each of the 2 corners. On the wrong side of the bib, align about 1" (2.5 cm) of one long edge of each twill tape tie with the second fold of the hem. Refold the hems and pin them in place. The opposite ends of the ties should extend beyond the top hemmed edge of the bib onto your work surface. With matching thread, topstitch the hems in place, ⅜" (1 cm) from the outside edge, and backtack multiple times at the top end to secure the twill tape ties. These ties will be used to tie the apron around your neck **(FIGURE 1)**.

35 On each of the two 26" (66 cm) lengths of twill tape, turn one end under ½" (1.3 cm), then another ½" (1.3 cm). On the wrong side of the apron, at the point where the angle of the bib meets the vertical side edges, place the finished ends of the ties on

the right-hand and left-hand sides of the apron. Pin and then topstitch them in place, making a square to secure the ties **(FIGURE 1)**. Tie an overhand knot in the loose ends of each of the 4 ties.

36 Lay the 2" × 21" (5 × 53.5 cm) fabric D accent border strip across the bottom edge of the apron, with right sides together, and aligning the raw edges at the bottom of the apron. The two short sides of the border strip will extend beyond the width of the towel. Pin and then stitch these pieces together along the bottom edge. Press the seam allowances toward the border strip.

37 To hem the side edges of the border strip, press ½" (1.3 cm) toward the wrong side of the strip. Make sure the folded edges align with the side edges of the apron. If not, adjust the fold to match, then press again.

38 Press a ½" (1.3 cm) hem on the remaining long raw edge of the border strip. Fold the border strip over to the wrong side of the apron. Align the long edge that you just pressed so that it rests about ⅛" (3 mm) above the previously stitched seam line. Make sure the hemmed side edges of the border strip remain folded to the inside so the raw edges are covered. Pin in place from the right side.

39 Turn the apron over to the right side and pin the hemmed apron edges in place. To finish the border, with matching thread, edgestitch the short sides of the border strip, beginning at the bottom edge of the right-hand side of the apron. Pivot at the corner where the side of the border meets the top of the border. Stitch in the ditch to catch the folded edge of the border on the wrong side of the apron. When you reach the opposite corner, pivot, then edgestitch the side hem in place.

Add the Apron Pocket

40 Place the 7¾" × 9" (19.5 × 23 cm) fabric B Apron Pocket rectangle right-side up on your work surface. The 9" (23 cm) sides will be the top and bottom edges of the pocket.

41 Referring to the photo on page 11, position the remaining Pears and Leaves in the center of the rectangle. Make sure you leave 1¼" (3.2 cm) of empty space between the appliqués and the top

and side edges of the rectangle and 1" (2.5 cm) of empty space between the appliqués and the bottom edge. When you are pleased with your arrangement, remove the paper backing and fuse the pieces in place.

42 Freehand draw the pear stems onto the rectangle and on the outside of the Pear Centers with light pencil lines.

43 Blanket-stitch around the Pears and Leaves as you did on the Pear Tea Towel (Step 24). Chain-stitch the pear stems as you did in Step 25.

44 With right sides together and the raw edges aligned, pin, then sew the 1¼" × 9" (3.2 × 23 cm) Pocket Accent strip (fabric D) to the top of the appliquéd Pocket rectangle. Press the seam allowances toward the Accent strip. You have completed the Pocket front.

45 With right sides together and the raw edges aligned, pin the 8½" × 9" (21.5 × 23 cm) Pocket Lining rectangle (fabric C) to the appliquéd Pocket front. Beginning on the bottom edge of the pocket, sew the pieces together around the edges, leaving a 3" (7.5 cm) opening at the bottom for turning.

46 Trim the corners and turn the pocket right-side out, using a point turner or chopstick to push out the corners. Press the pocket flat. Fold the seam allowances at the opening to tuck them inside. Press the pocket flat.

47 Position the pocket where you want it on the front of the apron and pin in place. In the sample, the pocket is located about 5¼" (13.5 cm) from each side edge of the apron and 12½" (31.5 cm) from the top edge of the apron. Pin in place.

48 Using matching thread, edgestitch the pocket in place, down the first side, across the bottom, and up the next side. Do not stitch the accent strip at the top of the pocket to the apron. Be sure to backtack at the beginning and end of the stitch line to secure the sides. ✑

- - - - - - - - - - - - - - - - - - - -

JENNIFER REYNOLDS is an Australian quilt and textile designer, regularly published in Australian quilting and stitchery magazines. She heads the Gum Tree Designers, a group of five Australian designers, all of whom annually design quilts and sewn projects for charity. Visit her website at elefantz.com.

Templates are actual size

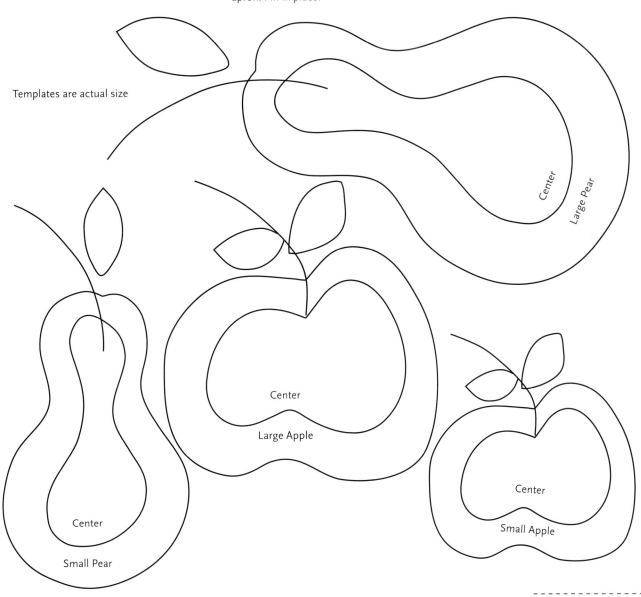

Large Pear
Center

Small Pear
Center

Large Apple
Center

Small Apple
Center

Fabric-Covered Notepads

BY MEGAN SMITH

Finding the perfect gift is hard, but making the perfect gift can be even harder. A gift that is useful to the recipient, as well as stylish and quick to make, is a rare combination.

Materials

☐ Fabric for the front, 10" × 11" (25.5 × 28 cm) rectangle

☐ Fabric for the lining, 10" × 11" (25.5 × 28 cm) rectangle

☐ Fabric for the inside pocket, 4½" × 8" (11.5 × 20.5 cm)

☐ Batting, 10" × 11" (25.5 × 28 cm) rectangle

☐ ⅜" (1 cm) wide elastic to hold the notepad, ¼ yd (23 cm) length

☐ Button, ¾"–1" (2–2.8 cm) diameter

☐ Narrow ribbon or cording for the closure, ¼ yd (23 cm) length

☐ Notepad, 4" × 8" (10 × 20.5 cm; these are available at most craft stores)

☐ Materials for embellishing (needle and thread, stamps and ink, stencils, etc.)

Finished Size

5" × 9" (12.5 × 23 cm)

Note

✳ To make a cover for another size notepad, calculate the fabric and lining rectangle sizes as follows. For the width, multiply the width of the notepad by 2 and add 2" (5 cm). For the length, add 3" (7.5 cm) to the length of the notepad.

Directions

1 Embellish the right side of the front fabric rectangle with quilting, needle-work, stamping, or any technique of your choice. Keep in mind the center fold and ½" (1.3 cm) seam allowance when planning your embellishment.

2 Press the pocket fabric side and bottom edges under ½" (1.3 cm). Press the top edge under in a doubled ½" (1.3 cm) hem and topstitch it in place. Position the pocket on the right side of the lining fabric, 1¼" (3.2 cm) from the left edge and 2½" (6.5 cm) from the top edge; pin it in place. Topstitch the side and bottom edges of the pocket to the lining.

3 Cut (2) 4¼" (11 cm) long strips of elastic. Pin 1 strip across the right half of the lining, 1½" (3.8 cm) from the top edge and ¾" (2 cm) from the right edge. Pin the second strip 2" (5 cm) from the bottom edge and ¾" (2 cm) from the right edge.

4 Use a wide zigzag stitch and a short stitch length to securely stitch all 4 of the elastic ends to the lining. Slide the cardboard back of the notepad through the elastic strips and make sure it fits snugly. If not, zigzag stitch again, making the opening a bit smaller. Remove the notepad and set it aside.

5 Place the embellished front right-side up on the batting. Sew the button in place through both layers, ¾" (2 cm) from the right edge and 5" (12.5 cm) from the top edge.

6 Wrap the ribbon or cording around the button and, adding 2" (5 cm) to the length for overhang, cut the ribbon. Fold it in half to make a loop, then tack the ribbon together 1" (2.5 cm) from the ends.

7 Pin the lining to the front fabric with right sides together and the batting on the bottom. Measure 5" (12.5 cm) from the top on the left edge and pin the looped ribbon between the front and lining layers with the 1" (2.5 cm) ends extending outward and the loop lying between the front fabric and lining.

8 Sew the layers together, stitching around the perimeter with a ½" (1.3 cm) seam allowance and leaving a 2" (5 cm) opening for turning. Trim the corners. Turn the notepad cover right-side out and press, pressing the opening seam allowances under. Check to see if the ribbon wraps nicely around the button and adjust if needed. Topstitch around the edges, stitching the opening closed.

9 Insert the notepad and enjoy! 🖋

- -

MEGAN SMITH can be found online at hiphome.blogspot.com.

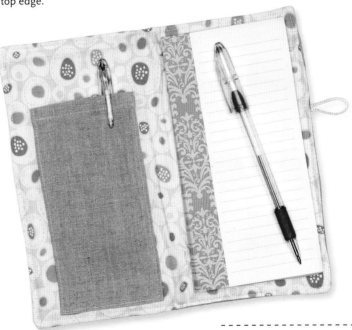

Artful Eco Bags

BY KELLI PERKINS

We've all become more aware of the impact of plastic grocery bags on the environment. The kindest thing we can do is to replace them with a reusable alternative. Why not make a boodle of fabric replacement bags, customized for your recipient? You can whip them up in no time, so plan to make a few for yourself as well. The best part is that you can roll them up and tuck them into your purse or glove box, so they're always handy for impromptu market strolls. If they get soiled, pop them in the washing machine and they're ready for the next trip.

Materials

☐ 1 yd (91.5 cm) printed cotton fabric

☐ 24" (61 cm) matching grosgrain ribbon

☐ Machine thread

☐ Template on page 20

Optional

☐ Plain canvas

☐ Fabric paint and paintbrush, if you want to paint, stamp, or stencil your own designs onto your bag

Directions

1 Cut 2 each of bag body and facing.

2 Turn under ¼" (6 mm) along the long bottom edge of a facing piece 2 times and zigzag stitch to finish it. Repeat with the other facing.

3 Place a bag body and facing right sides together and pin in place. Using a ½" (1.3 cm) seam, stitch around the bag top, from side seam to side seam (but not sewing the side seams), leaving the very top of each handle open. Repeat with the other bag body and facing. Clip all curves and turn each piece right-side out, then iron.

4 Fold the ribbon in half, locate the center of one bag side, and pin the ribbon to the bag body (fabric right-side up) so that the long pieces are toward the center of the bag and the folded edge aligns with the raw edge.

5 Place 2 bag bodies right sides together with the facing flipped up and pin. Stitch around the entire perimeter of the bag, from the edge of the facing piece, down the side, bottom, other side, and through to the end of the other side facing.

6 Make a gusset in each bottom corner by aligning the bottom seam with a side seam and opening the seam allowances flat. Sew straight across the corner about 1½" (3.8 cm) in from the tip. Repeat for the second gusset. Zigzag stitch the interior seam allowances to finish. Turn the bag right-side out and press.

7 Secure the facing to the inside by stitching down each side seam from the top of the bag to the end of the facing, using a zigzag stitch and coordinating thread.

8 With the bag turned right-side out and the facing on the inside, sew straight across each pair of handles, 1½" (3.8 cm) down from the top. Trim one of the 1½" (3.8 cm) flaps to ¼" (6 mm), and fold the raw edge. Fold the raw edge of the other flap under ¼" (6 mm), and pin it over the trimmed edge. Topstitch around the created rectangle.

9 To add letter blocks, cut some pieces of plain cotton canvas to whatever size you'd like. With black fabric paint, stamp block letters onto the canvas, then highlight them with a coordinating color of paint in a random stipple. Allow the paint to dry and then iron to set.

10 Dab the letters with a glue stick to temporarily hold them in place while you position them. When you're satisfied, zigzag stitch around the canvas to attach the fabric blocks. With a coordinating color of thread, free-motion stitch around each stamped letter.

11 To roll up a bag, lay it out on a table, text-side up. Fold the handles down, fold the top down, and then fold the bottom up so that the ribbon is centered on the side. On the side opposite the ribbon, begin rolling up the bag jelly roll style and then tie it with the ribbon. 🍃

- - - - - - - - - - - - - - - - - - - -

KELLI PERKINS shares her artistic journey through her blog at ephemeralalchemy.blogspot.com.

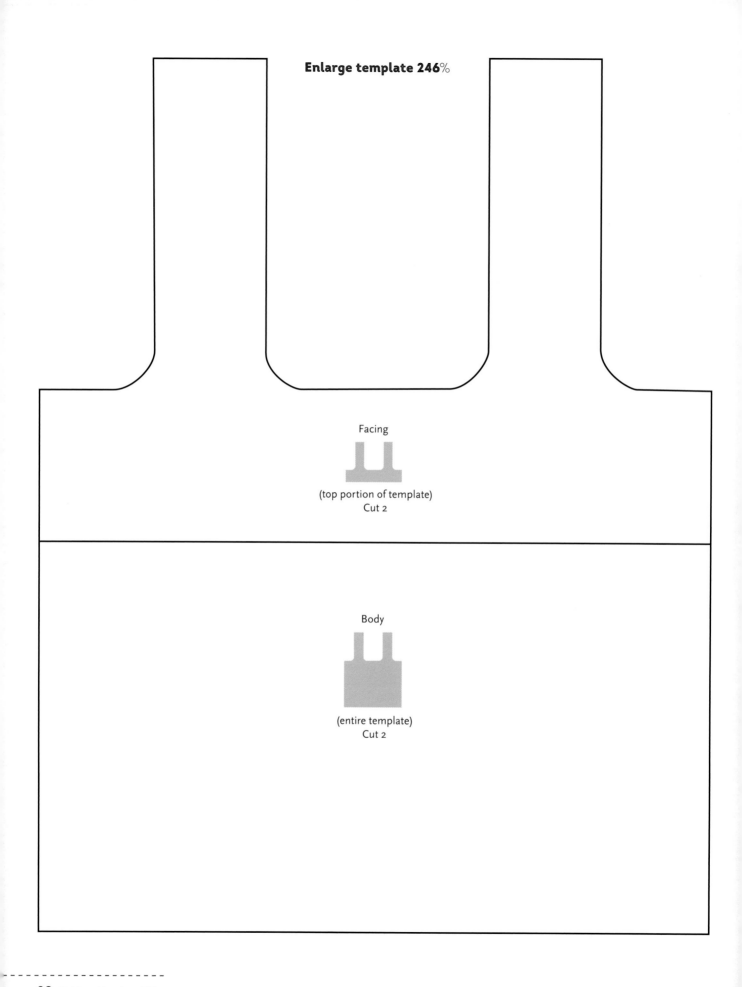

Enlarge template 246%

Facing

(top portion of template)
Cut 2

Body

(entire template)
Cut 2

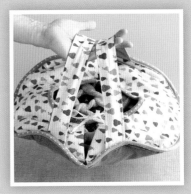

Potluck Take-Along

BY MELISSA FRANTZ

This cozy little carrier makes arriving with your dish intact at your next potluck or picnic a snap. It is adjustable to fit around one- to three-quart dishes snugly—just tighten the drawstring as far as it will go and the carrier will shrink around your dish!

Materials

- ☐ ½ yd (46 cm) of woven cotton or linen for Bottom (at least 45" [114.5 cm] wide; fabric A)

- ☐ ½ yd (46 cm) of woven cotton or linen in a contrasting color for Top and Straps (at least 45" [114.5 cm] wide; fabric B)

- ☐ ½ yd (46 cm) of low-loft quilt or thermal batting

- ☐ Coordinating sewing thread

- ☐ 2 yd (1.8 m) of coordinating ½" (1.3 cm) wide double-fold bias tape

- ☐ 30" (76 cm) of ¼" (6 mm) wide twill tape

- ☐ Potluck Take-Along template on page 23

- ☐ Rotary cutter and self-healing mat

- ☐ Bodkin or small safety pin for threading the drawstring

Finished Size

14" (35.5 cm) in diameter

Notes

* All seam allowances are ½" (1.3 cm) unless otherwise noted.

* To speed the construction, you might try using pre-quilted, double-sided fabric instead of using separate fabrics for the shell and lining of the Top and Bottom pieces and sewing together the layers. You might also try using ⅛" (3 mm) wide elastic or ribbon instead of twill tape for the drawstring.

Cut Out Fabric

1. Fold each fabric in half widthwise, right sides together, so you are cutting two layers at a time. Using the provided template on page 23 and scissors or a rotary cutter, trace and cut out the following pieces as directed (remember, you will be cutting 2 pieces at a time; the numbers given below are the total pieces needed):

   — Cut 2 Bottoms from fabric A.

   — Cut 1 Bottom from batting.

   — Cut 4 Tops and 4 Straps from fabric B.

   — Cut 2 Tops from batting.

Assemble Top and Straps

2. Place two Top pieces right sides together and then lay one piece of Top batting on top, aligning all edges, and pin all layers together. Sew together along the two short sides and smaller interior curved side, leaving the longest outer curved edge open. Trim the corners and clip the seam allowances on the curves. Turn right-side out and push out the corners; press flat. Repeat the entire step with the remaining Top pieces. Repeat with the remaining Top pieces. You now have the completed tops. Place the pieces so that they are facing each other as mirror images and make a light mark or place a pin on each to indicate that these are the right sides of each piece.

3. Create your drawstring casing by attaching bias tape to the interior curved side on each top piece. *First, fold one short edge of the bias tape ½" (1.3 cm) toward the wrong side and press. Now, tuck one of the top pieces inside the bias tape by about ¼" (6 mm), beginning with the folded-under edge of the bias tape at one end of the interior curve of the top piece. Pin the bias tape in place along this edge, taking care that only ¼" (6 mm) of the top piece is tucked inside the bias tape along the length (make sure that the right [marked] side of the top piece is facing up). Stop pinning about 1" (2.5 cm) before the end of the curved edge and trim the bias tape ½" (1.3 cm) from the edge of the top piece. Fold the extra ½" (1.3 cm) to the wrong side as before and finger-press. Finish pinning the bias tape in place. Edgestitch the bias tape in place, leaving the short edges open to allow the drawstring to pass through later. Stitch slowly, checking often that the underside of the bias tape is being caught in the stitching as well. Repeat from * to create the drawstring casing on the remaining top piece.

4. Place two of the Strap pieces right sides together and pin. Sew the long edges of the strap with a ¼" (6 mm) seam allowance, leaving each short edge open. Turn right-side out and press flat. Topstitch ⅛" (3 mm) from each long edge, down the length of the straps. Repeat the entire step to create the other strap.

Assemble the Layers

5. Stack the layers in the following order: one Bottom piece (right-side down), Bottom batting, remaining Bottom piece (right-side up), both assembled top pieces (right-side up, one on each side and with equally spaced gaps between pairs of short edges), both Straps (right-side up, matching the Straps' notches to the Tops' notches).

6. Pin all layers together. As you work with the thick stack of fabrics and batting, make sure the overall shape stays true to the original circle pattern piece and pin the pieces together. Ease the pieces slightly if necessary and don't be afraid to use a lot of pins.

7. Machine baste all the layers together as close to the edge as possible. Check to be sure you have caught all the layers in the basting stitches and remove all pins. Trim the Straps to match the circle's edge, if necessary. Alternatively, you can set the machine for a zigzag stitch 5.0 mm wide and 2.0 mm long and zigzag over the circle edges rather than using a traditional basting stitch. The zigzag will compress the edges, making it easier to bind them.

8. Slip the circle's outer edge into the bias tape, snugging it up into the center crease, and pin in place around the entire circle. Stop pinning about 2" (5 cm) before you reach the starting point and trim the bias tape to fit, leaving an extra 1" (2.5 cm). Turn ½" (1.3 cm) of the bias tape toward the wrong side and finger-press. Finish pinning the bias tape in place, lapping the folded end over the starting edge of the bias tape. Edgestitch the bias tape around the entire circle, stitching slowly and checking often to make sure that the underside of the bias tape is being caught in the stitching as well.

9. Finally, thread the twill tape through both of the casings on the interior curves of the top pieces, using a bodkin to guide the twill tape through. To use a safety pin, simply attach the safety pin to one end of the twill tape and then insert the safety pin into one of the casings and work it along with your fingers until it comes out the other side; repeat to continue through the other casing. Make an overhand knot near each end of the twill tape. To use the carrier, simply pull the top flaps aside to place the dish inside and pull the drawstring to tighten the top flaps around the dish. Use the handles to carry your dish and you're ready to go! 🍃

- -

MELISSA FRANTZ lives and sews in Portland, Oregon, with her family. She writes about all these things at allbuttonedup.typepad.com.

Enlarge all templates 200%

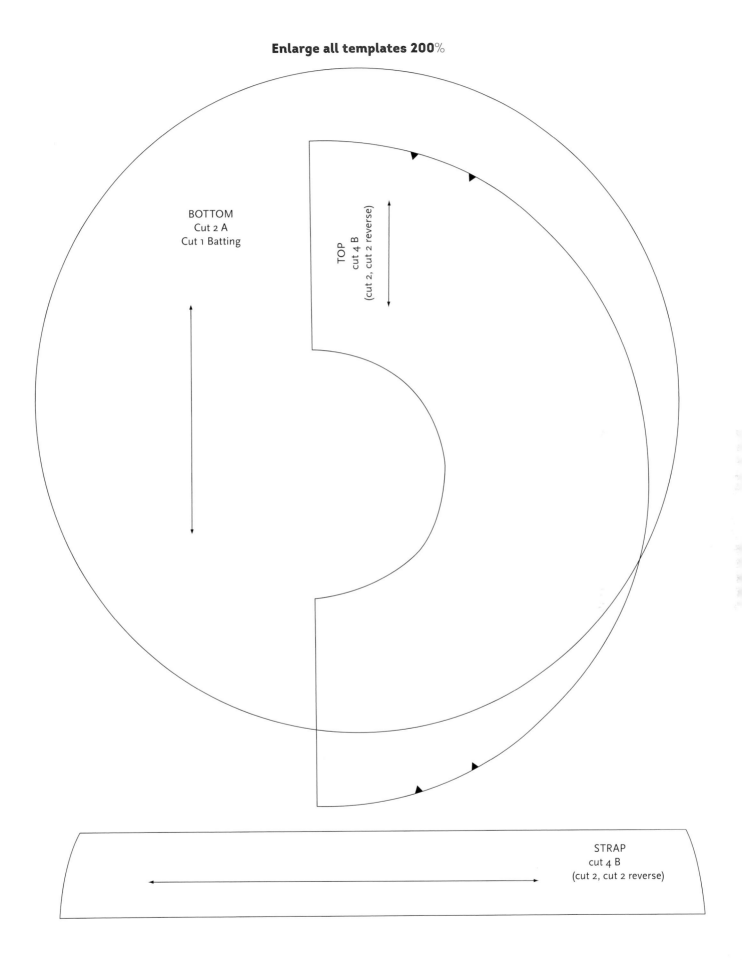

BOTTOM
Cut 2 A
Cut 1 Batting

TOP
cut 4 B
(cut 2, cut 2 reverse)

STRAP
cut 4 B
(cut 2, cut 2 reverse)

Journal Cover with a Zipper Pocket

BY VALORI WELLS

A handmade fabric cover adds a delightful touch to an everyday journal, and this cover goes one step further: it includes a zippered pocket for convenient storage of your journaling tools. Now you'll never be without your favorite pencils! For the exterior of my journal cover, I used a piece of home-dec weight screen-printed fabric; the lining is a bright floral print from my "Wrenly" fabric collection with FreeSpirit.

Materials

Fits a 5½" × 8½" (14 × 21.5 cm) journal

☐ Fabric for exterior: 1 rectangle 10" × 15" (25.5 × 38 cm), 1 rectangle 3" × 10" (7.5 × 25.5 cm)

☐ Fabric for lining, 1 rectangle 10" × 18½" (25.5 × 47 cm)

☐ Fabric for pocket, 2 rectangles 4½" × 10" (11.5 × 25.5 cm; I used the same fabric as the lining.)

☐ Interfacing (mid-weight, fusible on one side), 1 rectangle 10" × 15" (25.5 × 38 cm), 1 rectangle 3" × 10" (7.5 × 25.5 cm)

☐ 7" (18 cm) zipper

☐ 5½" × 8½" (14 × 21.5 cm) journal

Note

✳ Use ¼" (6 mm) seams throughout. These instructions will make a cover to fit a 5½" × 8½" (14 × 21.5 cm) journal. If you wish to make a cover for a different-sized journal, adjust the measurements as needed.

Directions

1 Fuse the interfacing rectangles to the wrong side of the same-sized exterior fabric rectangles.

2 Layer the large interfaced exterior fabric rectangle (right-side up), the zipped zipper (right-side down and centered along a 10" [25.5 cm] edge), and 1 pocket rectangle (right-side down and aligned along the same edge). Pin. Using a zipper foot and a ⅜" (1 cm) seam allowance, stitch the layers together.

3 Open the piece and press both fabrics away from the zipper teeth (so the wrong sides of the fabrics are together). With the exterior fabric faceup, edge-stitch along the zipper.

4 In the same manner, layer, pin, and sew the remaining exterior fabric rectangle and pocket rectangle to the other side of the zipper. Press and edgestitch.

5 Match the pocket fabrics so the right sides are together. Stitch around the 3 open edges of the pocket to close it.

6 Place the exterior fabric rectangle flat on your work surface, right-side up, with the zipper and narrow exterior fabric strip all placed out flat and right-side up. The pocket will be underneath; position it so it's under the large rectangle.

7 Layer the lining fabric rectangle on the front fabric, right sides together; trim the lining if necessary. Stitch around all 4 edges, leaving an opening for turning along 1 long side. Clip the corners and turn the piece right-side out through the opening. Turn the seam allowance along the opening to the inside; press.

8 Topstitch the short sides only.

9 To create the flaps, fold 2½" (6.5 cm) to the lining side at each end and pin to hold (the zipper should be along the fold of 1 flap). To secure the zipper fold, topstitch from the top of the piece just down to the top of the zipper, backtacking at both ends. Do the same at the bottom of the zipper.

10 Topstitch along the top and bottom edges of the cover, securing the flaps in the seam and being sure to catch the unstitched seam allowance of the opening used for turning the piece.

11 Insert your journal and your writing/drawing tools and enjoy! 🖊

- -

Find VALORI WELLS online at valoriwells.com.

Handy Sack

BY JIL CAPPUCCIO

Zipped up it looks like a wallet, but unzip it and out pops a handy, sturdy, and adorable tote bag! Have fun mixing fabric prints and zipper colors for a unique look.

Materials

☐ ¾ yd (68.5 cm) of lightweight cotton print (Main; shown: brown/white polka dot)

☐ ¼ yd (23 cm) of twill, denim, or printed canvas (Contrast; shown: pink/red/cream floral canvas)

☐ 14" (35.5 cm) or longer contrasting zipper

☐ Coordinating sewing thread

☐ Handy Sack template on page 29

Finished Size

Unzipped bag: 13½" × 6" × 10" (34.5 × 15 × 25.5 cm)

Zipped-up wallet: 6" × 4½" (15 × 11.5 cm)

Notes

✻ All seam allowances are ⅝" (1.5 cm) unless otherwise noted.

✻ French seams were used to make the bag sturdy and finished both inside and out; you can use a serger or zigzag or overlock stitch if you prefer and just trim off the extra seam allowance.

Cut the Fabric

1 Cut the following pieces as directed, using the provided patterns or dimensions (where dimensions are given, no pattern is provided). Transfer all markings and notches to the fabric.

From the Main fabric, cut:

— 1 Sack Body on the fold (mark both raw edges at fold line)

— Two 18" × 4½" (45.5 × 11.5 cm) pieces for the Handles

From the Contrast fabric, cut:

— One 9¾" × 6¼" (25 × 16 cm) piece for the Wallet

Make the Wallet/Sack Bottom

2 Fold the Wallet piece in half widthwise, right sides together, and press to crease. With the Wallet piece right-side up and starting at the crease, pin the zipper wrong side flush with the raw edge of the Wallet piece, folding the top end of the zipper tape out on the diagonal. Start stitching (using a ¼" [6 mm] seam allowance) the zipper to within ¼" (6 mm) of the first corner and stop with the needle in the down position. Pivot and continue to stitch the zipper to the next corner and finally to the center crease, again folding the end of the zipper tape out on the diagonal **(FIGURE 1)**.

3 Fold the Wallet right sides together and stitch the remaining zipper tape along the raw edges of the other half of the

Wallet. Unzip the Wallet and turn it right-side out; this will be the bottom of your sack.

Make the Sack

4 Lay the Sack Body piece right-side up and pin the wallet right-side up on the Sack Body, aligning the wallet's corners with the markings and turning the seam allowance (and zipper edge) under the wallet. Edgestitch the wallet to the sack, following the perimeter of the wallet and making sure the stitching catches the seam allowance and zipper edges between the wallet and the sack fabric.

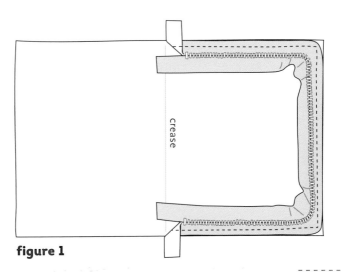

crease

figure 1

5 Sew the side seams, using French seams (see sidebar on page 28) if desired.

6 Match each side seam with the corresponding fold line mark (from Step 1) on the sack bottom and use French seams to finish the bottom of the sack.

7 Press all seams. Press the top edge of the sack under ½" (1.3 cm), then press under another ½" (1.3 cm) for the top hem.

8 Fold each Handle piece in half lengthwise and press. Open it up and press each long edge under to meet the center crease. Refold each Handle along the initial crease and edges-stitch to close the folds. Your Handles should be about 1" (2.5 cm) wide when you are finished.

9 Insert the raw ends of one Handle into the top hem fold on one side of the sack, matching the ends with the notches. Pin the Handles in place and topstitch near the hem fold to finish the top of the sack. The handles will be hanging on the inside of the sack.

10 Now flip the handles up and stitch them to the top of the hem fold, reinforcing the stitching by sewing back and forth several times to make sure the handles are sturdily secured.

Press the top hem and handles. To use, fold the sack flat into the wallet and zip the wallet closed around it to keep the bag contained and compact until needed. 🍃

- - - - - - - - - - - - - - - - - - -

JIL CAPPUCCIO has been a designer, seamstress, and shop owner for twenty years. For more information, visit her website, jilcappuccio.com.

French Seams

This seam-finish technique encloses the seam allowance, leaving behind only finished edges on the inside and out. It's a great option for sheer or very lightweight fabrics to hide raw edges in see-through garments. For the version shown here, a ⅝" (1.5 cm) wide seam allowance is used.

1 Lay your fabrics on top of each other with their wrong sides together and raw edges aligned. Sew the seam with a ⅜" (1 cm) seam allowance.

2 Trim the seam allowance to ⅛" (3 mm). To prevent raveling, be careful not to cut into your stitches or cut too close to the seam line. [a]

3 Press the seam line flat to set the stitches. Then press the seam allowance open from the wrong side. Next, fold the fabric along the seam line with right sides together. [b]

4 Sew the seam again, stitching ¼" (6 mm) from the seamed edge. [c]

5 Press the seam allowance to one side to finish. [d]

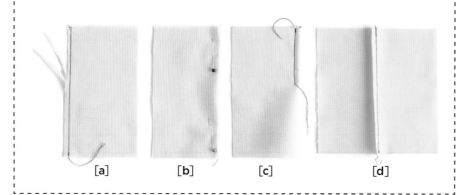

[a]   [b]   [c]   [d]

Enlarge template 250%

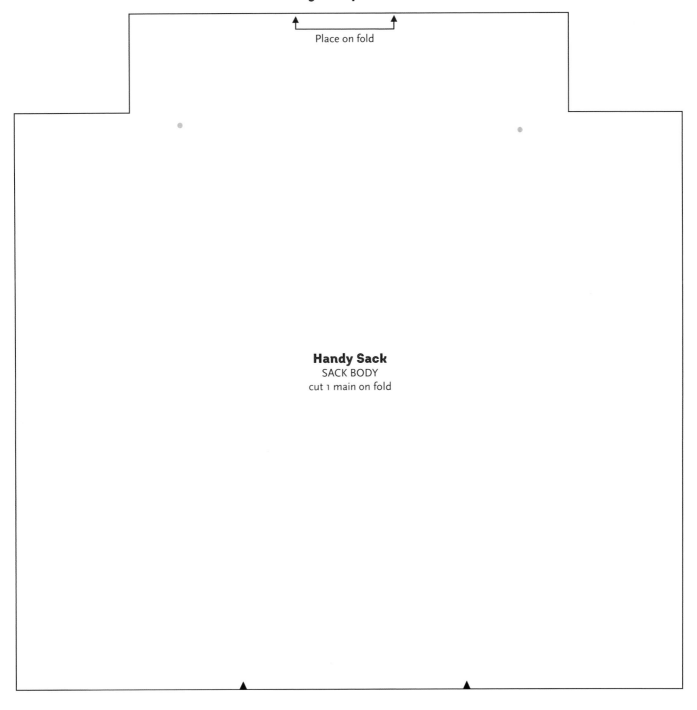

Place on fold

Handy Sack
SACK BODY
cut 1 main on fold

Patchwork Pot Holder

BY KAELIN TELSCHOW

This is a great way to use up scraps or precut squares left over from a previous project. The fussy-cut center is also perfect for creating a themed or seasonal pot holder. I've been using this pattern to make one for each major holiday!

Materials

- ☐ Twelve 2" (5 cm) print squares
- ☐ 2" (5 cm) fussy-cut square (for the center)
- ☐ Two 1¼" × 3½" (3.2 × 9 cm) solid sashing strips
- ☐ Two 1¼" × 2" (3.2 × 5 cm) solid sashing strips
- ☐ 7" (18 cm) square piece of backing fabric
- ☐ 7" (18 cm) square piece of thermal batting
- ☐ 2½" (6.5 cm) piece of linen or twill tape (for the hook tab)
- ☐ Package of ½" (1.3 cm) bias tape

Directions

1 Sew the 1¼" × 2" (3.2 × 5 cm) sashing strips to the top and bottom of the fussy-cut center square. Once attached, sew the 1¼" × 3½" (3.2 × 9 cm) sashing strips to the sides.

2 Lay your 12 remaining squares around the center piece until you find an arrangement that you like. There should be 4 squares in the top and bottom rows and 2 squares on the sides.

3 Piece the squares into rows and attach them to the center piece, starting with the smaller side strips.

4 Layer your top, batting, and backing as you would a quilt, cut off the excess, and quilt together.

5 Before binding, flip the pot holder over to the back side. Lay the linen tape diagonally about 1" (2.5 cm) out from the top left corner. Pin in place and trim the excess tape that hangs over the edges. Bind (the binding will secure the hook tab in place). 🖋

Visit **KAELIN TELSCHOW**'s blog at theplaidscottie.blogspot.com.

Materials

- ☐ ⅜ yd (34 cm) of 45" (115 cm) wide linen or other neutral base fabric
- ☐ ¼ yd (23 cm) of 45" (115 cm) wide cotton print fabric for piecing and oven mitt lining
- ☐ Assorted scraps at least 2½" × 2½" (6.4 × 6.4 cm)
- ☐ ⅜ yd (34 cm) of cotton batting
- ☐ ⅜ yd (34 cm) of heat-resistant batting (shown here: Insul-Bright)
- ☐ 2 yd (1.8 m) of extra-wide double-fold bias tape
- ☐ Sewing thread to match linen or base fabric
- ☐ Sewing thread to match bias tape
- ☐ Vintage or new buttons of your choice (shown here: two ⅞" [23 mm] buttons to embellish the pot holder, and two ⅝" [15 mm] buttons layered over two 1¼" [32 mm] buttons to embellish the oven mitt)
- ☐ Pot holder pattern templates on page 33
- ☐ Rotary cutter and self-healing cutting mat
- ☐ Acrylic quilting ruler
- ☐ Assorted machine needles: sizes 80/12, 90/14, and/or 100/16

Finished Size

Oven mitt: 11" × 7" (28 × 18 cm)
Pot holder: 6½" (16.5 cm) square

Notes

* Use a ¼" (6 mm) seam allowance for piecing and a ½" (1.3 cm) seam allowance for sewing.

* You can make the oven mitt more fitted in the thumb, fingers, and palm area, while leaving the wrist wider to show off more of the piecing design, bracelet-style, but you can streamline the wrist to be more fitted, if you like.

* Ideally, use a size 80/12 or 90/14 machine needle for piecing and a size 90/14 or 100/16 needle to sew the layers of fabric and batting together.

Pieced Pot Holders

BY SUSAN BEAL

Easy-to-make pot holders are a fun way to use small amounts of cute prints and solids for random piecing on a natural linen background. Edging the pieces with bright bias tape and adding contrast buttons brings the simple design to life.

Cut Out Fabric

1 Using the patterns provided on page 33, cut out the following pieces:

— **Oven mitt:** Cut two pieces from the linen for the outer layer, two pieces from the contrast print for the lining, two pieces from the batting, and two pieces from the heat-resistant batting.

— **Pot holder:** Cut two pieces from the linen for the outer layer, one piece from the batting, and one piece from the heat-resistant batting.

2 To prepare the linen pieces, cut along the solid lines transferred from the pattern pieces and discard the fabric between the lines. Leave the lining, batting, and heat-resistant batting pieces intact.

3 Cut two 5" (12.7 cm) pieces of bias tape (which will later become loops on your pot holder and oven mitt) and edgestitch (see Sewing Basics) both long edges of each one through all layers.

Prepare Piecing Strips

4 Prepare your print fabrics for the random-length piecing by cutting each one into pieces 2½" (6.5 cm) wide and 1"–4" (2.5–10 cm) long. Arrange the pieces side by side so that adjoining pieces always differ. Using a ¼" (6 mm) seam allowance, join the strips together one by one to form a strip 28"–30" (71–76 cm) long. Press the seams to one side.

5 Cut the strip of random-length piecing into four sections, each about 7" (18 cm) long, two each for the oven mitt and pot holder.

Create the Pieced Outer Sections

6 Pin one strip of piecing to the edge of one narrow pot-holder section, right sides together, and stitch, using a ¼" (6 mm) seam allowance. Press the seam toward the pot holder. Pin the opposite side of the piecing strip to the wider pot-holder section, right

sides together, checking to make sure the pot-holder sections align across the pieced strip. Stitch a ¼" (6 mm) seam and press the seam allowances toward the pot holder. Trim the excess pieced strip so it is flush with the pot-holder edges.

7 Repeat Step 6 to assemble the second outer pot holder.

8 Repeat Step 6 again to assemble the two outer oven mitts.

Layer Sections and Quilt Piecing

9 Layer one outer pot holder, right-side up, on top of the corresponding heat-resistant batting, and the second outer piece, right-side up, on top of the standard batting. Pin the stacks together in several places.

10 Lay one oven mitt lining on the work surface, right-side down. Top it with a layer of batting, a layer of heat-resistant batting, and one outer oven mitt piece, right-side up. Repeat to form a second stack with the remaining oven mitt pieces, making sure the thumb position is reversed in the second stack. Pin the stacks together in several places.

11 Using a contrasting or neutral thread color, stitch in the ditch (see Sewing Basics) between the various contrasting fabric patches and along the edges of the pieced strips on each layered pot holder and oven mitt unit. Backtack at the beginning and end of each seam, and quilt each of the four units the same way. The pot-holder units will be relatively thin (two layers each) and the oven mitt units will be thick (four layers each).

Assemble the Pot Holder

12 To create the pot holder, stack the two quilted units, right-sides out, raw edges aligned, and pin. Baste around the perimeter in a neutral color, ¼" (6 mm) from the edge. Trim the edges, if necessary, to neaten and square the pot holder.

13 Beginning near the center of one side, encase the raw edges with bias tape. Miter each corner (see Sewing Basics), or round the corners by tracing around a large spool and cutting along the line to avoid the need to miter. Edgestitch near the bias edge, checking frequently to ensure the binding edge on the pot holder's other side is also caught by the stitches. Stop sewing just before returning to the beginning point, trim the bias tape 1" (2.5 cm) beyond the beginning, and turn ½" (1.3 cm) to the wrong side. Finish sewing the binding to the pot holder, lapping the folded end over the beginning raw edge.

Assemble the Oven Mitt

14 Baste around the perimeter of each oven mitt unit separately in a neutral color, ¼" (6 mm) from the edge. Trim the edges, if necessary, to neaten.

15 Cut two 8" (20 cm) pieces of bias tape to cover the wrist edges of each oven-mitt section. Encase the wrist edges in the bindings, centering the quilted pieces on the bias tape, and edgestitch each with coordinating thread, but do not trim the extra tape yet.

16 Stack the two quilted layers, right sides together, and pin. Stitch the two layers together, using a 3.0 mm stitch length, leaving the bound wrist edge and the first 1" (2.5 cm) of the outer side seam (opposite the thumb side) open. Trim the seam allowance to ¼" (6 mm) except along the 1" (2.5 cm) left open at the side, and reinforce the seam with a zigzag, overcasting, or serger stitch. Turn the mitt right-side out.

Add Loops and Buttons

17 To finish the pot holder, create a loop with one of the two pieces of bias tape you stitched in Step 3. Arrange it at one upper corner as shown on the pattern, with one end of the loop on each side of the pot holder, and baste. Sew on a ⅞" (2.2 cm) button to cover and secure the loop ends on each side.

18 To finish the oven mitt, fold the remaining loop in half. Align the loop with the bias binding at the wrist, tucking the loop ends inside the open seam. Finish sewing the open seam, backtacking securely, and catching the loop ends in the seam. Fold the seam allowances open and whipstitch (see Stitch Glossary) the loop ends to the inside of the wrist binding on either side of the seam.

19 Stack the ⅝" (15 mm) and 1¼" (32 mm) buttons, creating two layered ornaments, and sew one on each side of the mitt at the base of the loop.

- -

SUSAN BEAL is a writer and crafter in Portland, Oregon. She is the author of *Bead Simple* and *Button It Up*. Visit her website: westcoastcrafty.com.

Enlarge both templates 200%

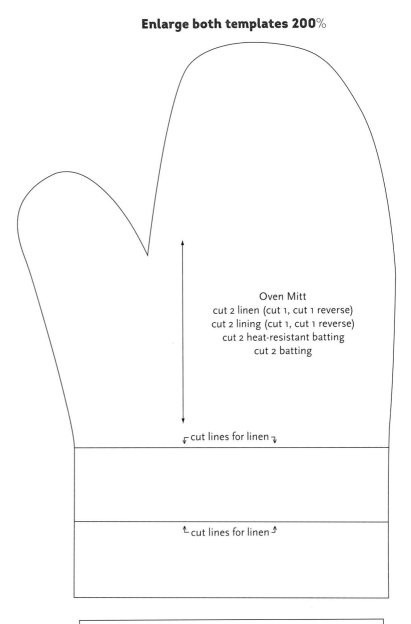

Oven Mitt
cut 2 linen (cut 1, cut 1 reverse)
cut 2 lining (cut 1, cut 1 reverse)
cut 2 heat-resistant batting
cut 2 batting

↳cut lines for linen↲

↳cut lines for linen↲

Pot Holder
cut 2 linen (cut 1, cut 1 reverse)
cut 2 batting (cut 1, cut 1 reverse)
cut 1 heat-resistant batting

↳cut lines for linen↲

↳cut lines for linen↲

Nested Storage Boxes

BY LUCIE SUMMERS

Make pretty little boxes to keep all your small sewing notions or other assorted bric-a-brac beautifully organized. Make a nesting set in coordinating fabrics or just one to hold tiny treasures.

Materials

- [ ] About ¼ yd (23 cm) each (or desired scraps) of 8 different 45" (114.5 cm) wide print fabrics (see Notes)
- [ ] Polyester sewing threads to blend with all fabrics
- [ ] Sharps handsewing needle
- [ ] Curved upholstery needle (optional)
- [ ] Mat board, about 1/16" (2 mm) thick, two 16" × 20" (40.5 × 51 cm) sheets or one 32" × 40" (81.5 × 101.5 cm) sheet
- [ ] Glue stick
- [ ] Rotary cutter, rigid acrylic ruler, and self-healing mat
- [ ] Metal ruler or other straightedge (optional)
- [ ] Craft knife for cutting mat board
- [ ] Thimble (optional)
- [ ] Binder clips or clothespins

Finished Sizes

Large Box: 6" (15 cm) square × 5" (12.5 cm) high; Medium Box: 5" (12.5 cm) square × 4" (10 cm) high; Small Box: 4" (10 cm) square × 3" (7.5 cm) high; Tiny Box: 3" (7.5 cm) square × 2" (5 cm) high

Notes

* Most of the fabrics used for the sample boxes are from the Nature Walk organic fabric line by Cloud9 fabrics, cloud9fabrics.com. The prints used were: Grove in colors Straw and Sky; Leaves in colors Crimson and Leaf; Clearing; and Moss in colors Ocean, Earth, and Crimson.

* This project is perfect for fat eighths, fat quarters, 10" (25.4 cm) precut squares, and (for pieced sides or smaller boxes) 5" (12.5 cm) precut charm squares.

* Mat board, chipboard, or gray board is a great weight for this project, light yet sturdy for a really professional feel. A cereal box or thin card works well too, although one layer might be a little flimsy; try gluing two pieces together. You could also use an ultra-firm interfacing (such as Timtex); if you think it's a little thin, use two pieces together.

* On some of the boxes, the fabric is pieced together to create a patchwork effect. This is very easy to do—simply randomly stitch scraps of your chosen fabrics together using a ¼" (6 mm) seam allowance and press the seams open. Trim the patchwork to the desired size (see Cut the Fabric) and make the box as directed.

* If you decide to make a patchwork box, make the bottom of the box using a solid piece of fabric to prevent a wobbly box.

* Even if you don't usually use a thimble for handsewing, try it with with this project because stitching the box together is a tricky task without one.

* A curved upholstery needle can simplify whipstitching the box corners together.

* Following are the instructions for a basic fabric box, but remember, you can really go to town and decorate the box in any way you'd like. Embellish with embroidery, appliqué, beads, you name it! Remember, you will need to decorate the fabric before gluing it to the mat board and constructing the box.

Cut the Fabric

Note: Cut the shell and lining pieces from any of the print fabrics, deciding which fabrics you'd like to feature in each location on each box before cutting. Label each piece with the box size and the location (e.g., "Large shell side" or "Medium lining bottom") as you cut. Organize the pieces for each box in a separate pile or in a labeled plastic bag to avoid confusion.

1 For the large box, cut:

— Four 6" × 5" (15 × 12.5 cm) pieces for the shell sides

— One 6" × 6" (15 × 15 cm) piece for the shell bottom

— Four 6" × 5" (15 × 12.5 cm) pieces for the lining sides

— One 6" × 6" (15 × 15 cm) piece for the lining bottom

2 For the medium box, cut:

— Four 5" × 4" (12.5 × 10 cm) pieces for the shell sides

— One 5" × 5" (12.5 × 12.5 cm) piece for the shell bottom

— Four 5" × 4" (12.5 × 10 cm) pieces for the lining sides

— One 5" × 5" (12.5 × 12.5 cm) piece for the lining bottom

3 For the small box, cut:

— Four 4" × 3" (10 × 7.5 cm) pieces for the shell sides

— One 4" × 4" (10 × 10 cm) piece for the shell bottom

— Four 4" × 3" (10 × 7.5 cm) pieces for the lining sides

— One 4" × 4" (10 × 10 cm) piece for the lining bottom

4 For the tiny box, cut:

— Four 3" × 2" (7.5 × 5 cm) pieces for the shell sides

— One 3" × 3" (7.5 × 7.5 cm) piece for the shell bottom

— Four 3" × 2" (7.5 × 5 cm) pieces for the lining sides

— One 3" × 3" (7.5 × 7.5 cm) piece for the lining bottom

Cut the Mat Board

Note: Half of the pieces cut for each size box will be used for the lining and will need to be trimmed slightly. However, the exact dimensions depend on fabric and board thickness and can't be determined until the box shell has been stitched together.

When cutting mat board with a craft knife, a metal ruler or straightedge is a more reliable guide than an acrylic ruler, which can be cut by the knife blade.

5 For the large box, cut:

— Eight 5" × 4" (12.5 × 10 cm) pieces for the sides

— Two 5" × 5" (12.5 × 12.5 cm) pieces for the bottoms

6 For the medium box, cut:

— Eight 4" × 3" (10 × 7.5 cm) pieces for the sides

— Two 4" × 4" (10 × 10 cm) pieces for the bottoms

7 For the small box, cut:

— Eight 3" × 2" (7.5 × 5 cm) pieces for the sides

— Two 3" × 3" (7.5 × 7.5 cm) pieces for the bottoms

8 For the tiny box, cut:

— Eight 2" × 1" (5 × 2.5 cm) pieces for the sides

— Two 2" × 2" (5 × 5 cm) pieces for the bottoms

Assemble the Boxes

Follow the instructions below for each box.

9 Lay out all of the fabric (wrong-sides up) and mat board pieces for the shell of one box, including the pieces for the bottom of the box. For the moment, put the fabric and mat board lining pieces to one side.

10 Spread glue generously over one side of each piece of mat board.

11 Center each piece of mat board on the wrong side of its corresponding fabric piece. Turn the board over and make sure the fabric is smooth, without puckers or pleats.

12 Turn the board back over to the wrong side. Beginning with the shorter sides, spread glue along the edges of the visible fabric, fold the fabric edges neatly over the board, and press down firmly. Do the same with the long sides. When folding at the corners, tuck a little extra fabric between the fabric and board and pull the fabric taut to create a smooth, sharp corner (**FIGURE 1**). Repeat with the remaining box sides and bottom. Leave the pieces to dry.

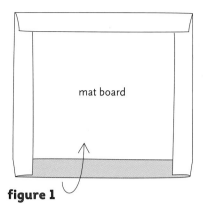

figure 1

13 Place one box side on the box bottom, wrong sides together, and whipstitch the edges securely together by hand. Keep the stitches as small and neat as possible because they will be seen! After every few stitches, stand the box side on end as it will be positioned in the finished box and check the stitch tension: too tight and the side won't stand perpendicular to the bottom; too loose and the stitches will be too prominent. Stitch the remaining side panels to the other edges of the box bottom, creating a cross shape (**FIGURE 2**).

14 Fold the box sides upward to form the box, with the stitches acting as hinges, and whipstitch each side panel to its neighbors as before. Begin each seam at the top edge of the box and work toward the bottom; if one side of the box is slightly larger than its neighbor, it's easier to hide. This is the exciting part as the box begins to take shape.

Line the Boxes

15 Carefully measure the inside of the box in two ways: across the top of the box between the inside surfaces of opposite side panels for one measurement and from the bottom to the top of the box interior for the other. Scribble with a pencil on the back (visible mat board side) of the measured side to remind yourself which piece you have already measured, because each side may be slightly different.

16 Transfer the measurements to one piece of lining mat board. You may find you just need to trim the tiniest amount off for a correct fit; a very rough estimate is $1/16$" (2 mm). The goal is to

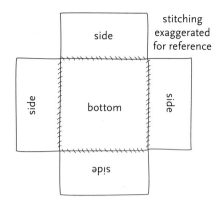

figure 2

have the box lining at the same height or a little lower than the corresponding box side. After trimming, place the board inside the box to check the fit and adjust its size further if necessary. It should be very slightly loose, to allow for fabric thickness.

17 Cover the lining mat board with a piece of lining fabric as in Step 12 and check the fit again while the glue is still wet, to allow further size adjustments if necessary. Spread glue generously on the wrong side of the lining panel and adhere it inside the box, using binder clips or clothespins to hold it in place while the glue dries.

18 Repeat Steps 16 and 17 with the next lining side, measuring and gluing the lining to the opposite box side.

19 Repeat Steps 16 and 17 with the remaining two lining sides and finally the box bottom (measure across the box in both directions, between the inside surfaces of the lining side pieces, to determine the bottom's dimensions). Use clothespins to hold the lining sides in place and place a small heavy object in the box to keep the bottom flat. Leave the box to dry completely. 🍃

- -

LUCIE SUMMERS is a designer/maker from the United Kingdom, where she lives on a farm with her family in the Suffolk countryside. She designs and screen prints fabrics for sale at her online shop under her Summersville label. She regularly exhibits her work at The Festival of Quilts in Birmingham, where she has won several prizes. See her fabric at etsy.com/shop/summersville.

Materials

- ☐ Two 18" × 18" (45.5 × 45.5 cm) pieces of patterned cotton fabric for body of bag (fabric A)
- ☐ Two 34" × 3" (86.5 × 7.5 cm) pieces of patterned cotton fabric for straps (fabric A)
- ☐ Two 18" × 18" (45.5 × 45.5 cm) pieces of patterned cotton fabric for small pockets (fabric B)
- ☐ Two 23" × 18" (58.5 × 45.5 cm) pieces of patterned cotton fabric for large pockets (fabric B)
- ☐ Two 14" × 18" (35.5 × 45.5 cm) pieces of contrasting cotton fabric for lining
- ☐ Two 34" × 2½" (86.5 × 6.5 cm) pieces of medium-weight fusible interfacing for straps
- ☐ Contrasting sewing thread
- ☐ 12" (30.5 cm) of embroidery thread, any color
- ☐ Size 3 embroidery needle
- ☐ Fabric pencil
- ☐ Long knitting needle, any size
- ☐ Rotary cutter and self-healing cutting mat
- ☐ Acrylic ruler

Finished Size

Body of bag: 17" × 13" (43 × 33 cm)

Length with straps: 26¼" (66.5 cm)

Take-Along Tote

BY MELINDA BARTA

Whether toting your sewing supplies to class or craft night, you'll fit all of your necessities in this stylish, large-pocketed sewing bag. Mix boldly patterned fabrics together for an inspired look.

Make Pockets

1 Fold one 23" × 18" (45.5 × 58.5 cm) piece of fabric B in half widthwise with wrong sides facing and press the fold. Sew ½" (1.3 cm) from the end of the fold (this fold will be the top edge of the pockets). Repeat entire step three times using the remaining pieces of fabric B.

2 Lay one 18" × 18" (45.5 × 45.5 cm) piece of fabric A right-side up on your worktable. Lay 1 large piece of fabric B then 1 small piece of fabric B, on top of fabric A. Align the layers so that the 18" (45.5 cm) raw edges of the folded fabrics align with the bottom edge of fabric A. Pin the layers. Mark vertical lines using the marking pencil over all layers at 2½", 6½", 11½", and 15½" (6.5, 16.5, 29, and 39.5 cm) from the left edge. Sew through all layers along the marked lines to create pockets **(FIGURE 1)**. Repeat stitching so each line has two passes of stitching less than ⅛" (3 mm) apart. Remove pins. Repeat entire step with the remaining pieces of fabric.

Make Body of Bag

3 With right sides together and using a ½" (1.3 cm) seam allowance, join the sides and bottom edges of the 2 layered fabrics created in Step 2. Cut one 2"× 2" (5 × 5 cm) square out of the bottom left corner of the layers. Repeat in the bottom right corner **(FIGURE 2)**. Open the body of the bag and refold so that the bottom seam is in line with one side seam at the left corner (the raw edges created by the square that was just removed will be aligned). Sew along the raw edges using a ½" (1.3 cm) seam allowance to form the bottom corner of the bag **(FIGURE 3)**. Repeat at opposite corner.

4 Turn the bag right-side out. Fold the top ¾" (2 cm) of the bag toward the inside of the body (wrong sides together), press, and sew ½" (1.3 cm) from the fold.

Make Lining

5 Repeat Step 3 using the two pieces of lining fabric (instead of the fabrics layered in Step 2). Insert the lining into the body of the bag so that

wrong sides are together. Fold the top 3½" (9 cm) of the body toward the inside of the bag, over the lining (the top edge of the lining will be nestled in the fold). Pin the lining to the body in several places. Sew around the top edge of the bag ½" (1.3 cm) from the folded edge, then sew another line 2" (5 cm) from the folded edge (1½" [4 cm] from the first stitched line).

Make Straps

6 Center 1 piece of interfacing, fusible side down, on the back of 1 long strip of fabric A and fuse according to manufacturer's directions. Fold the strip in half lengthwise with right sides together. Sew, using a ½" (1.3 cm) seam allowance, to form a tube.

7 Use 16" (40.5 cm) of embroidery thread and the needle to take a few stitches near one corner of the tube; remove the needle and tie the working and tail threads around the base of the knitting needle. Pass the knitting needle through the tube to turn it inside out. Cut the embroidery thread and press the tube so the seam runs down the middle. Sew down the length of the tube, ¼" (6 mm) from one folded edge. Repeat along the other folded edge. Repeat both stitched lines, stitching less than ⅛" (3 mm) away, inside the previous lines.

8 Repeat Steps 6 and 7 for second strap. Fold each end of one strap over, so both raw edges are on the same side facing away from the seam, and sew down ¼" (6 mm) from the fold. Fold and stitch the second strap in the same manner. Pin the straps in place inside the bag so that the raw edges of the folds just stitched face the bag (the straps here were centered between the seam lines of the 4" [10 cm] wide pockets located on either side of the center pockets). Sew in place in a free-form manner using several passes of relatively straight lines.

9 Sew around the bag ¼" (6 mm) from the top edge. 🍃

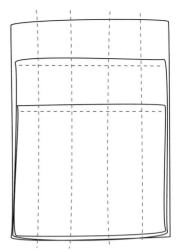

figure 1

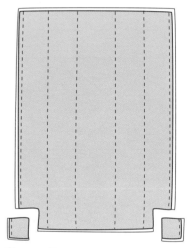

figure 2

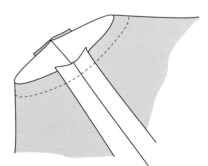

figure 3

- -

MELINDA BARTA is the editor of *Beadwork* magazine and author of *Custom Cool Jewelry*, *Hip to Stitch*, and *Mixed Metals*. Visit her website: melindabarta.com.

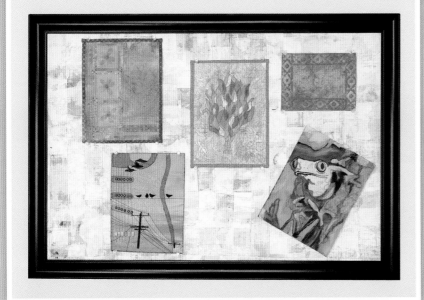

Patchwork Design Wall

BY POKEY BOLTON

Some quilters like to simply cover a piece of foam core with felt to make a simple design wall, but I wanted to add a little patchwork interest to mine to decorate my quilt studio. When I'm not using it as a design wall, it can serve double duty as a bulletin board!

Materials

- ☐ Large frame without the glass (I went to the frame section of my craft store and bought the biggest one they had.)

- ☐ White and light-colored fabric (Patterned fabric adds interest, but make sure the patterns are low contrast.)

- ☐ Piece of foam core cut to size to fit inside the frame

- ☐ Gesso

- ☐ Black rubber-stamping ink

- ☐ Rubber stamps with bold, chunky designs

- ☐ Brayer

- ☐ PVA glue (such as Aleene's Tacky Glue or Sobo glue)

Directions

1. Cut 2½" × width of fabric strips.

2. Strip piece the long pieces together using a ¼" seam allowance. Continue to piece until your finished piece is larger than your foam core piece. Press the seam allowances open.

3. Lay your strip-pieced fabric onto your cutting mat so that the lengths are horizontally oriented and rotary cut crosswise into new 2½" strips.

4. Reposition the newly cut strips so different fabrics are next to each other.

5. Piece these new long strips together.

6. Stamp randomly all over.

7. Saturate your brayer with gesso and roll the brayer over various parts of the pieced fabric. Do not cover it entirely, but do roll over the stamped areas to tone down the black ink. Allow to dry.

8. Cover the foam core with the finished patchwork and glue into place so it is taut. Allow the glue to dry.

9. Insert into frame and hang. 🖋

POKEY BOLTON founded *Quilting Arts* Magazine, co-founded *Cloth Paper Scissors*, and is the host of *Quilting Arts TV.* She is currently the Chief Creative Officer at Quilts Inc.

Soft + Soothing Eye Pack

BY MISSY SHEPLER

This envelope-style eye mask has a secret inside—a pocket for a hot or cold pack! Treat yourself (or a friend) to a soft, soothing flannel-covered eye escape that's super-simple to make.

Materials

- [ ] 1 fat eighth (see Notes) of cotton flannel fabric for outer eye pack (Main; shown: white)

- [ ] Two 2¼" × 10" (5.7 × 25.4 cm) scraps of flannel fabric for contrast binding (Contrast; shown: light green)

- [ ] 1 fat eighth (see Notes) of cotton muslin for inner hot pack

- [ ] Heavyweight thread (28 weight) to match binding fabric for embellishment

- [ ] Matching sewing thread

- [ ] Handsewing needle

- [ ] Uncooked white rice or flaxseed and dried herbs of your choice for hot pack

- [ ] Rubbing alcohol (for optional cold pack)

- [ ] Quart-size freezer bag (for optional cold pack)

- [ ] Free-motion or darning foot for sewing machine

- [ ] Fabric marking pen

- [ ] Spray starch or tear-away stabilizer (optional)

- [ ] Softly Soothing Eye Pack template on page 42

Finished Size

About 8" × 4½" (20.5 × 11.5 cm)

Notes

* All seam allowances are ½" (1.3 cm) seam allowance unless otherwise noted.

* Prewash and press all fabrics.

* Fat eighths are fabric cuts often sold (alone or in color-coordinated sets) at fabric and quilt stores. Half the size of a fat quarter, a fat eighth can be either 9" × 22" (23 × 56 cm) or 11" × 18" (28 × 46 cm). If fat eighths are unavailable, purchase ¼ yd (23 cm) of fabric.

Embellish and Cut the Fabric

1. Trace and cut out the Eye Pack pattern and reserve the rest of the pattern sheet or paper to use as a placement window.

2. Set the sewing machine for free-motion stitching, lowering or covering the feed dogs. Using the heavyweight thread, freehand machine embroider a motif of your choice on the Main cotton flannel fabric; the sample is stitched with relaxing, swirling curves. Mark stitching lines on the flannel before beginning or let your imagination guide the needle as you sew. Take care to hold the flannel taut while stitching, so that the embroidery doesn't distort the fabric; starching the fabric or backing it with tear-away stabilizer will help. When stitching is complete, remove any stabilizer and markings used, washing and drying the fabric if necessary. Press the stitched fabric from the wrong side on a padded surface.

3. Lay the pattern outline (stencil remaining from cutting out the pattern) on the embellished fabric. Move this pattern window around on the fabric and choose the areas to use in the project.

4. Cut 2 Eye Pack pieces from the embellished flannel fabric for the outer eye pack, trimming one piece at the trim line as indicated on the pattern. If making a hot pack, cut 2 Eye Pack pieces from the muslin, using the appropriate cutting lines.

Make the Outer Eye Pack

5. Press ½" (1.3 cm) to the wrong side on one long edge of each binding strip.

6. Align the unpressed long edge of one binding strip with the straight edge of the shortened Main fabric Eye Pack piece, placing the right side of the binding strip against the wrong side of the Eye Pack. Pin and then sew the two pieces together along the straight edge.

7. Press the binding and seam allowances away from the eye pack. Fold the pressed binding edge over the seam allowances to the front of the pack;

the pressed edge should just cover the seam line. Edgestitch the binding fold, concealing the seam allowances. Trim the excess binding even with the sides of the Eye Pack. This is the eye pack front.

8. Repeat Steps 6 and 7 to attach the remaining binding strip to the second Eye Pack piece; this is the eye pack back.

9. With right sides together, align the eye pack pieces along the curved edges. The back eye pack piece is longer than the front. Pin together along the curved edges.

10. Fold the back's bound edge to the right side ⅛" (3 mm) above the front's bound edge, tucking the back bound edge between the back and front. The bindings will be staggered, lying side by side at the seam line. Pin the side edges. Stitch the pieces together along the side and curved edges.

11. Grade one seam allowance to ¼" (6 mm) and clip the curves though both fabric layers, taking care not to cut into the seam. Turn the assembled eye pack right-side out through the opening at the bound edge. The back's bound edge will lap over the front binding.

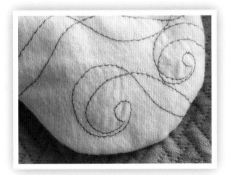

Make the Inner Hot Pack

12 With right sides together, align the two muslin Eye Pack pieces along all edges and pin. Using a ¼" (6 mm) seam allowance, sew around all edges, pivoting at the corners and leaving a 2" (5 cm) opening along the straight edge for turning.

13 Clip the corners and curves, taking care not to cut into the seam. Turn the assembled hot pack right-side out. Press, folding the edges along the 2" (5 cm) opening to the inside of the pack.

14 Fill the inner hot pack with uncooked rice or flaxseed. Don't overfill; the pack should be flexible enough to conform to your face. For a soothing scent, add a few tablespoons of your favorite dried herb or spice to the rice or flax. Slip-stitch the opening closed.

15 To use your hot pack, microwave the inner hot pack on high for 1 to 3 minutes. (Microwaves vary. Experiment to find what works best with your appliance.) Slip the warmed inner hot pack inside the outer eye pack and soothe the pain away!

Scent Suggestions

☐ Mint

☐ Lemon Balm

☐ Thyme

☐ Lavender

☐ Rose Petals

☐ Cinnamon

☐ Cloves

☐ Nutmeg

☐ Rosemary

Make an Ice Pack (Optional)

Alcohol ice packs are fast and easy to make, with ingredients you may already have on hand.

16 Place one part rubbing alcohol to two parts water in a sealable quart-size freezer bag. Squeeze as much air out of the bag as you can, then seal the bag in a second freezer bag, to guard against leaks.

17 Place the bag in the freezer for several hours or overnight. The alcohol will keep the water from freezing into a solid. For a slushier ice pack, reduce the amount of alcohol in the mix. To use your ice pack, just slip the plastic bag inside the outer eye pack and keep cool! ✿

- -

MISSY SHEPLER is the coauthor of the *Complete Idiot's Guide to Sewing*. Whenever possible, Missy combines her day job as a designer, author, and illustrator with her love of stitching by creating projects, patterns, and illustrations for sewing and quilting clients and publications.

Enlarge template 166%

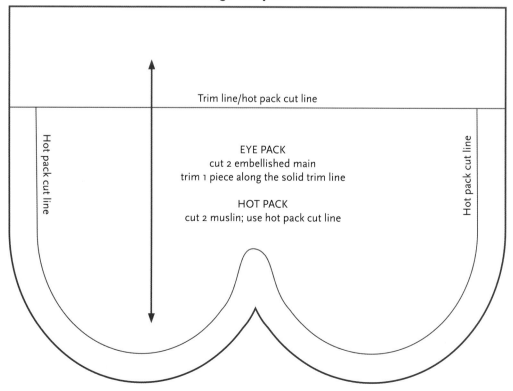

Trim line/hot pack cut line

Hot pack cut line

EYE PACK
cut 2 embellished main
trim 1 piece along the solid trim line

HOT PACK
cut 2 muslin; use hot pack cut line

Hot pack cut line

Sewing Basics

A quick reference guide to basic tools, techniques, and terms

For all projects (unless otherwise indicated):

* When piecing: Use ¼" (6 mm) seam allowances. Stitch with the right sides together. After stitching a seam, press it to set the seam; then open the fabrics and press the seam allowance toward the darker fabric.

* Yardages are based upon 44" (112 cm) wide fabric.

Sewing Kit

The following items are essential for your sewing kit. Make sure you have these tools on hand before starting any of the projects:

* **ACRYLIC RULER** This is a clear flat ruler, with a measuring grid at least 2" × 18" (5 × 45.5 cm). A rigid acrylic (quilter's) ruler should be used when working with a rotary cutter. You should have a variety of rulers in different shapes and sizes.

* **BATTING** 100% cotton, 100% wool, plus bamboo, silk, and blends.

* **BONE FOLDER** Allows you to make non-permanent creases in fabric, paper, and other materials.

* **CRAFT SCISSORS** To use when cutting out paper patterns.

* **EMBROIDERY SCISSORS** These small scissors are used to trim off threads, clip corners, and do other intricate cutting work.

* **FABRIC** Commercial prints, hand-dyes, cottons, upholstery, silks, wools; the greater the variety of types, colors, designs, and textures, the better.

* **FABRIC MARKING PENS/PENCILS + TAILOR'S CHALK** Available in several colors for use on light and dark fabrics; use to trace patterns and pattern markings onto your fabric. Tailor's chalk is available in triangular pieces, rollers, and pencils. Some forms (such as powdered) can simply be brushed away; refer to the manufacturer's instructions for the recommended removal method for your chosen marking tool.

* **FREE-MOTION OR DARNING FOOT** Used to free-motion quilt.

* **FUSIBLE WEB** Used to fuse fabrics together. There are a variety of products on the market.

* **GLUE** Glue stick, fabric glue, and all-purpose glue.

* **HANDSEWING + EMBROIDERY NEEDLES** Keep an assortment of sewing and embroidery needles in different sizes, from fine to sturdy.

* **IRON, IRONING BOARD + PRESS CLOTHS** An iron is an essential tool when sewing. Use cotton muslin or silk organza as a press cloth to protect delicate fabric surfaces from direct heat. Use a Teflon sheet or parchment paper to protect your iron and ironing board when working with fusible web.

* **MEASURING TAPE** Make sure it's at least 60" (152.5 cm) long and retractable.

* **NEEDLE THREADER** An inexpensive aid to make threading the eye of the needle superfast.

* **PINKING SHEARS** These shears have notched teeth that leave a zigzag edge on the cut cloth to prevent fraying.

* **POINT TURNER** A blunt, pointed tool that helps push out the corners of a project and/or smooth seams. A knitting needle or chopstick may also be used.

* **ROTARY CUTTER + SELF-HEALING MAT** Useful for cutting out fabric quickly. Always use a mat to protect the blade and your work surface (a rigid acrylic ruler should be used with a rotary cutter to make straight cuts).

* **SAFETY PINS** Always have a bunch on hand.

* **SCISSORS + SHEARS** Heavy-duty shears reserved for fabric only; a pair of small, sharp embroidery scissors; thread snips; a pair of all-purpose scissors; pinking shears.

* **SEAM RIPPER** Handy for quickly ripping out stitches.

* **SEWING MACHINE** With free-motion capabilities.

* **STRAIGHT PINS + PINCUSHION** Always keep lots of pins nearby.

* **TEMPLATE SUPPLIES** Keep freezer paper or other large paper (such as parchment paper) on hand for tracing the templates you intend to use. Regular office paper may be used for templates that will fit. You should also have card stock or plastic if you wish to make permanent templates that can be reused.

* **THIMBLE** Your fingers and thumbs will thank you.

* **THREAD** All types, including hand and machine thread for stitching and quilting; variegated; metallic; 100% cotton; monofilament.

* **ZIPPER FOOT** An accessory foot for your machine with a narrow profile that can be positioned to sew close to the zipper teeth. A zipper foot is adjustable so the foot can be moved to either side of the needle.

Glossary of Sewing Terms and Techniques

BACKSTITCH Stitching in reverse for a short distance at the beginning and end of a seam line to secure the stitches. Most machines have a button or knob for this function (also called backtack).

BASTING Using long, loose stitches to hold something in place temporarily. To baste by machine, use the longest straight stitch length available on your machine. To baste by hand, use stitches at least ¼" (6 mm) long. Use a contrasting thread to make the stitches easier to spot for removal.

BIAS The direction across a fabric that is located at a 45-degree angle from the lengthwise or crosswise grain. The bias has high stretch and a very fluid drape.

BIAS TAPE Made from fabric strips cut on a 45-degree angle to the grainline, the bias cut creates an edging fabric that will stretch to enclose smooth or curved edges. You can buy bias tape ready-made or make your own.

CLIPPING CURVES Involves cutting tiny slits or triangles into the seam allowance of curved edges so the seam will lie flat when turned right-side out. Cut slits along concave curves and triangles (with points toward the seam line) along a convex curve. Be careful not to clip into the stitches.

CLIP THE CORNERS Clipping the corners of a project reduces bulk and allows for crisper corners in the finished project. To clip a corner, cut off a triangle-shaped piece of fabric across the seam allowances at the corner. Cut close to the seam line but be careful not to cut through the stitches.

DART This stitched triangular fold is used to give shape and form to the fabric to fit body curves.

EDGESTITCH A row of topstitching placed very close (¹⁄₁₆"–⅛" [2–3 mm]) to an edge or an existing seam line.

FABRIC GRAIN The grain is created in a woven fabric by the threads that travel lengthwise and crosswise. The lengthwise grain runs parallel to the selvedges; the crosswise grain should always be perpendicular to the lengthwise threads.

If the grains aren't completely straight and perpendicular, grasp the fabric at diagonally opposite corners and pull gently to restore the grain. In knit fabrics, the lengthwise grain runs along the wales (ribs), parallel to the selvedges, with the crosswise grain running along the courses (perpendicular to the wales).

FINGER-PRESS Pressing a fold or crease with your fingers as opposed to using an iron.

FUSSY-CUT Cutting a specific motif from a commercial or hand-printed fabric. Generally used to center a motif in a patchwork pattern or to feature a specific motif in an appliqué design. Use a clear acrylic ruler or template plastic to isolate the selected motif and ensure that it will fit within the desired size, including seam allowances.

GRAINLINE A pattern marking showing the direction of the grain. Make sure the grainline marked on the pattern runs parallel to the lengthwise grain of your fabric, unless the grainline is specifically marked as crosswise or bias.

INTERFACING Material used to stabilize or reinforce fabrics. Fusible interfacing has an adhesive coating on one side that adheres to fabric when ironed.

LINING The inner fabric of a garment or bag, used to create a finished interior that covers the raw edges of the seams.

MITER Joining a seam or fold at an angle that bisects the project corner. Most common is a 45-degree angle, like a picture frame, but shapes other than squares or rectangles will have miters with different angles.

OVERCAST STITCH A machine stitch that wraps around the fabric raw edge to finish edges and prevent unraveling. Some sewing machines have several overcast stitch options; consult your sewing machine manual for information on stitch settings and the appropriate presser foot for the chosen stitch (often the standard presser foot can be used). A zigzag stitch can be used as an alternative to finish raw edges if your machine doesn't have an overcast stitch function.

PRESHRINK Many fabrics shrink when washed; you need to wash, dry, and press all your fabric before you start to sew, following the suggested cleaning method marked on the fabric bolt (keep in mind

that the appropriate cleaning method may not be machine washing). Don't skip this step!

RIGHT SIDE The front side, or the side that should be on the outside of a finished garment. On a print fabric, the print will be stronger on the right side of the fabric.

RIGHT SIDES TOGETHER The right sides of two fabric layers should be facing each other.

SATIN STITCH (MACHINE) This is a smooth, completely filled column of zig-zag stitches achieved by setting the stitch length short enough for complete coverage but long enough to prevent bunching and thread buildup.

SEAM ALLOWANCE The amount of fabric between the raw edge and the seam.

SELVEDGE This is the tightly woven border on the lengthwise edges of woven fabric and the finished lengthwise edges of knit fabric.

SQUARING UP After you have pieced together a fabric block or section, check to make sure the edges are straight and the measurements are correct. Use a rotary cutter and an acrylic ruler to trim the block if necessary.

STITCH IN THE DITCH Lay the quilt sandwich right-side up under the presser foot and sew along the seam line "ditch." The stitches will fall between the two fabric pieces and disappear into the seam.

TOPSTITCH Used to hold pieces firmly in place and/or to add a decorative effect, a topstitch is simply a stitch that can be seen on the outside of the garment or piece. To topstitch, make a line of stitching on the outside (right side) of the piece, usually a set distance from an existing seam.

UNDERSTITCHING A line of stitches placed on a facing (or lining), very near the facing/garment seam. Understitching is used to hold the seam allowances and facing together and to prevent the facing from rolling toward the outside of the garment.

WRONG SIDE The wrong side of the fabric is the underside, or the side that should be on the inside of a finished garment. On a print fabric, the print will be lighter or less obvious on the wrong side of the fabric.

Stitch Glossary

BACKSTITCH

Working from right to left, bring the needle up at **1** and insert behind the starting point at **2**. Bring the needle up at **3**; repeat by inserting at **1** and bringing the needle up at a point that is a stitch length beyond **3**.

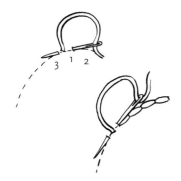

BASTING STITCH

Using the longest straight stitch length on your machine, baste to temporarily hold fabric layers and seams in position for final stitching. It can also be done by hand. When basting, use a contrasting thread to make it easier to spot when you're taking it out.

BLANKET STITCH

Working from left to right, bring the needle up at **1** and insert at **2**. Bring the needle back up at **3** and over the working thread. Repeat by making the next stitch in the same manner, keeping the spacing even.

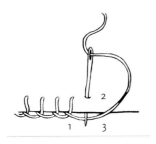

BLINDSTITCH/BLIND-HEM STITCH

Used mainly for hemming fabrics where an inconspicuous hem is difficult to achieve (this stitch is also useful for securing binding on the wrong side). Fold the hem edge back about ¼" (6 mm). Take a small stitch in the garment, picking up only a few threads of the fabric, then take the next stitch ¼" (6 mm) ahead in the hem. Continue, alternating stitches between the hem and the garment (if using for a non-hemming application, simply alternate stitches between the two fabric edges being joined).

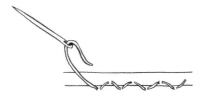

CHAIN STITCH

Working from top to bottom, bring the needle up at and reinsert at **1** to create a loop; do not pull the thread taut. Bring the needle back up at **2**, keeping the needle above the loop and gently pulling the needle toward you to tighten the loop flush to the fabric. Repeat by inserting the needle at **2** to form a loop and bring the needle up at **3**. Tack the last loop down with a straight stitch.

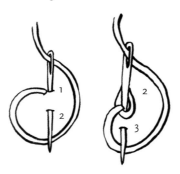

STRAIGHT STITCH + RUNNING STITCH

Working from right to left, make a straight stitch by bringing the needle up and insert at **1**, ⅛"–¼" (3–6 mm) from the starting point. To make a line of running stitches (a row of straight stitches worked one after the other), bring the needle up at **2** and repeat.

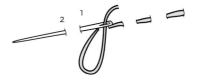

FRENCH KNOT

Bring the needle up at **1** and hold the thread taut above the fabric. Point the needle toward your fingers and move the needle in a circular motion to wrap the thread around the needle once or twice. Insert the needle near **1** and hold the thread taut near the knot as you pull the needle and thread through the knot and the fabric to complete.

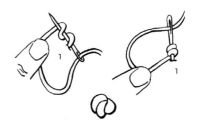

COUCHING

Working from right to left, use one thread, known as the couching or working thread, to tack down one or more strands of fiber, known as the couched fibers. Bring the working thread up at **1** and insert at **2**, over the fibers to tack them down, bringing the needle back up at **3**. The fibers are now encircled by the couching thread. Repeat to couch the desired length of fiber(s). This stitch may also be worked from left to right, and the spacing between the couching threads may vary for different design effects.

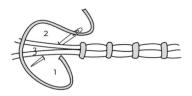

CROSS-STITCH

Working from right to left, bring the needle up at **1**, insert at **2**, then bring the needle back up at **3**. Finish by inserting the needle at **4**. Repeat for the desired number of stitches.

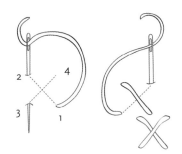

WHIPSTITCH

Bring the needle up at **1**, insert at **2**, and bring up at **3**. These quick stitches do not have to be very tight or close together.

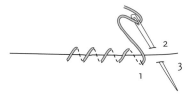

STANDARD HAND-APPLIQUÉ STITCH

Cut a length of thread 12"–18" (30.5–45.5 cm). Thread the newly cut end through the eye of the needle, pull this end through, and knot it. Use this technique to thread the needle and knot the thread to help keep the thread's "twist" intact and to reduce knotting. Beginning at the straightest edge of the appliqué and working from right to left, bring the needle up from the underside, through the background fabric and the very edge of the appliqué at **1**, catching only a few threads of the appliqué fabric. Pull the thread taut, then insert the needle into the background fabric at **2**, as close as possible to **1**. Bring the needle up through the background fabric at **3**, ⅛" (3 mm) beyond **2**. Continue in this manner, keeping the thread taut (do not pull it so tight that the fabric puckers) to keep the stitching as invisible as possible.

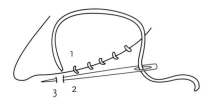

SLIP STITCH

Working from right to left, join two pieces of fabric by taking a ¹⁄₁₆"–¼" (2–6 mm) long stitch into the folded edge of one piece of fabric and bringing the needle out. Insert the needle into the folded edge of the other piece of fabric, directly across from the point where the thread emerged from the previous stitch. Repeat by inserting the needle into the first piece of fabric. The thread will be almost entirely hidden inside the folds of the fabrics.

Create Binding
CUTTING STRAIGHT STRIPS

Cut strips on the crosswise grain, from selvedge to selvedge. Use a rotary cutter and straightedge to obtain a straight cut. Remove the selvedges and join the strips with diagonal seams (see instructions at right).

CUTTING BIAS STRIPS

Fold one cut end of the fabric to meet one selvedge, forming a fold at a 45-degree angle to the selvedge (**1**). With the fabric placed on a self-healing mat, cut off the fold with a rotary cutter, using a straightedge as a guide to make a straight cut. With the straightedge and rotary cutter, cut strips to the appropriate width (**2**). Join the strips with diagonal seams.

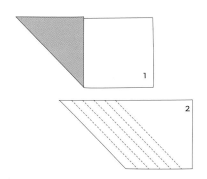

BINDING WITH MITERED CORNERS

Decide whether you will use a Double-fold Binding (option A at right) or a Double-layer Binding (option B at right). *If using double-layer binding follow the alternate italicized instructions in parenthesis.*

Open the binding and press ½" (1.3 cm) to the wrong side at one short end *(refold the binding at the center crease and proceed)*. Starting with the folded-under end of the binding, place it near the center of the first edge of the project to be bound, matching the raw edges, and pin in place. Begin sewing near the center of one edge of the project, along the first crease *(at the appropriate distance from the raw edge)*, leaving several inches of the binding fabric free at the beginning. Stop sewing ¼" (6 mm) before reaching the corner, backstitch, and cut the threads. Rotate the project 90 degrees to position it for sewing the next side. Fold the binding fabric up, away from the project, at a 45-degree angle (**1**), then fold it back

down along the project raw edge (**2**). This forms a miter at the corner. Stitch the second side, beginning at the project raw edge (**2**) and ending ¼" (6 mm) from the next corner, as before.

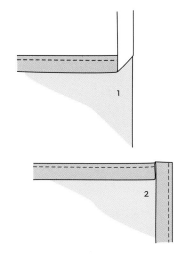

Continue as established until you have completed the last corner. Continue stitching until you are a few inches from the beginning edge of the binding fabric. Overlap the pressed beginning edge of the binding by ½" (1.3 cm) (or overlap more as necessary for security) and trim the working edge to fit. Finish sewing the binding *(opening the center fold and tucking the raw edge inside the pressed end of the binding strip)*. Refold the binding along all the creases and then fold it over the project raw edges to the back, enclosing the raw edges *(there are no creases to worry about with option B)*. The folded edge of the binding strip should just cover the stitches visible on the project back. Slip-stitch or blindstitch the binding in place, tucking in the corners to complete the miters as you go (**3**).

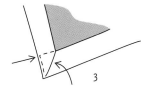

DIAGONAL SEAMS FOR JOINING STRIPS

Lay two strips right sides together, at right angles. The area where the strips overlap forms a square. Sew diagonally across the square as shown above. Trim the excess fabric ¼" (6 mm) away from the seam line and press the seam allowances open. Repeat to join all the strips, forming one long fabric band.

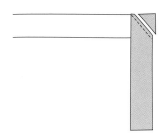

FOLD BINDING

A. Double-fold Binding

This option will create binding that is similar to packaged double-fold bias tape/binding. Fold the strip in half lengthwise, with wrong sides together; press. Open up the fold and then fold each long edge toward the wrong side, so that the raw edges meet in the middle (**1**). Refold the binding along the existing center crease, enclosing the raw edges (**2**), and press again.

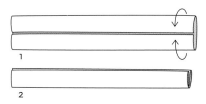

B. Double-layer Binding

This option creates a double-thick binding with only one fold. This binding is often favored by quilters. Fold the strip in half lengthwise with wrong sides together; press.

Find popular patterns for quick and easy projects with these *Craft Tree* publications, brought to you by Interweave.

Colorful Projects for Outdoor Fun

ISBN 978-1-62033-561-1

Easy Quilting Projects

ISBN 978-1-62033-556-7

Easy Sewing Projects

ISBN 978-1-62033-558-1

Great Projects for Guys

ISBN 978-1-62033-559-8

More Teacher Gifts

ISBN 978-1-62033-560-4

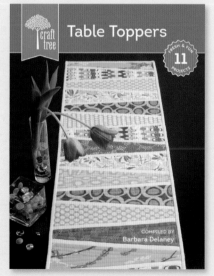

Table Toppers

ISBN 978-1-62033-557-4

Visit your favorite retailer or order online at interweavestore.com

INTERWEAVE.
interweavestore.com